An Amazing Journey

By Elizabeth Anne Brechter

HTP

Hidden Thoughts Press

This book is dedicated to all of my dear brothers and sisters who suffer with mental illness.

An Amazing Journey

Copyright © 2013 by Elizabeth Anne Brechter

First Edition

All Rights Reserved

ISBN 13: 978-0615922768
ISBN 10: 0615922767

Editor: Mary Harris
Cover: Pixellogic Studio / Joseph Sigillo
Cover Photo: Lorraine Kappus Correira
Layout: The Deliberate Page / Tamara Cribley

Printed in the United States

First Printing: November, 2013

1 2 3 4 5 6 7 8 9 10

HTP

www.HiddenThoughtsPress.com

Table of Contents

Acknowledgements i
Foreword. iii
Introduction v
Chapter One. 1
Chapter Two. 9
Chapter Three 15
Chapter Four 19
Chapter Five. 23
Chapter Six. 27
Chapter Seven 31
Chapter Eight. 37
Chapter Nine 39
Chapter Ten 43
Chapter Eleven. 47
Epilogue 53
Self-Help Mental Health Programs. 57

Acknowledgements

SARAH, MY CLOSEST FRIEND
Thank you for sticking by me for the past thirty-one years, as that is how long we have been friends. You have been a wonderful friend to me as you have always been there for me.

ASHLEY LEWIN, MY NATUROPATHIC DOCTOR AND CLOSE FRIEND
Thank you for guiding me as far as food is concerned for the past sixteen years, and you have been an amazing support to me.

DOROTHY REESE, MY FRIEND
I thank you for being in my life, as you are a real inspiration to me.

DOCTOR PETER KINGAN, MY PSYCHOLOGIST
Thank you for being my therapist for the past ten years, as you are the best therapist whom I have ever had.

MY PSYCHIATRIST (DOCTOR LONG IN AUTOBIOGRAPHY)
Thank you for being my psychiatrist for the past ten years, as you are the best psychiatrist I have ever had.

PROFESSOR WILBUR MILLER,
MY FORMER PROFESSOR AT STONY BROOK UNIVERSITY
Thank you for all your continued support throughout my school years at Stony Brook University.

PROFESSOR ALIX COOPER,
MY FORMER PROFESSOR AT STONY BROOK UNIVERSITY
Thank you for helping me to achieve the Writing Requirement at Stony Brook University.

PROFESSOR DONNA RILLING,
MY FORMER PROFESSOR AT STONY BROOK UNIVERSITY
Thank you for giving me a second chance with a failing essay that I wrote, and I ended up getting a B.

PROFESSOR JENNIFER ANDERSON,
MY FORMER PROFESSOR AT STONY BROOK UNIVERSITY
Thank you for being so sweet and kind to me.

DOCTOR NANCY TOMES,
MY FORMER PROFESSOR AT STONY BROOK UNIVERSITY
Thank you for helping me out with all of my essays.

DISABILITY SUPPORT SERVICES—STONY BROOK UNIVERSITY
Thank you for all your continued support throughout my school years at Stony Brook University.

STAFF AT FEDERATION OF ORGANIZATIONS, PATCHOGUE, NEW YORK
Thank you for all your support and kindness when I was working as a volunteer for your agency.

CATHOLIC CHARITIES, SUFFOLK COUNTY, NEW YORK
Thank you for your assistance, as your agency helped me get out of a violent and alcoholic home when I was twenty-two years old.

SUFFOLK COUNTY POLICE DEPARTMENT—FIFTH PRECINCT, PATCHOGUE, NEW YORK
When your officers took me to CPEP (Comprehensive Psychiatric Emergency Program) in 2003, they were very kind to me and treated me with respect and courtesy.

RESPONSE OF SUFFOLK COUNTY HOTLINE, NEW YORK
Thank you for being there for me when I needed you since 1972.

STAFF AT GOODYEAR SERVICE CENTER, CENTEREACH, NEW YORK
Thank you for always being honest with me about my car; you are such great friends to me.

STAFF AT ROBERTACCIO FUNERAL HOME, PATCHOGUE, NEW YORK
Thank you for being such good friends to me. I will always be grateful to you for burying my friend, Carmella, for not much money at all.

SACHEM LIBRARY, HOLBROOK, NEW YORK
Thank you for the use of your computers in order to complete my autobiography.

CHARLES DAY, MY FRIEND AND PUBLISHER
Thank you for all your support and for publishing my autobiography.

MARY HARRIS, MY EDITOR
Thank you for all your support and encouragement with my autobiography and thank you for editing it.

Foreword

The book you hold in your hand is aptly titled *An Amazing Journey*. Elizabeth Anne Brechter has written an honest and revealing account of what it is like to live with a serious mental illness. After you read it, you will be amazed at what she has overcome. I hope many people will read her story and appreciate the message of persistence, hope, and courage that she offers.

There are many lessons to be learned from Elizabeth's story, but what impressed me most was the testimony she provides about the power of the recovery model. As a historian of psychiatry, I would say that the recovery movement has probably done more to improve the lives of people with serious mental illness than any drug ever invented! From her first reading of Dr. Low's work, through her many years of involvement with AA, ACOA, OA, and other groups, Elizabeth has worked the program in order to heal herself. These pages testify to the long, hard work she has done: to learn to love and forgive herself, to make amends to people she has hurt, and to forgive those who have hurt her. She has done a remarkable job of learning to understand and manage the behaviors that put her at odds with herself and with other people. Elizabeth is the productive, creative, and vibrant person she is today because of her own hard work. Yes, as her story makes clear, she has been helped on that journey by good therapists, kind friends, and the wise use of medication and nutrition. But the secret to Elizabeth's recovery is her own strength. Faced with problems that would have sunk most of us, she never gave up trying to understand herself, and to get better.

I have been privileged to know Elizabeth during part of her amazing journey. I am one of the Stony Brook professors she mentions in her story. I can remember the first class I had with Elizabeth; she confided to me how anxious she was, speaking in class. But on a piece of paper, it was a different story! From the first time I asked her to write about history, she showed me that she had a gift for writing. What was hard for her to say out loud flowed on a piece of paper. In my class, she wrote feelingly about the life of the slave Harriet Tubman, a person who, like her, was born into a very difficult life yet survived to inspire others by her bravery. Reading Elizabeth's book now, I am struck by how she has used the telling of her own personal history as a way to come to terms with the past. She has used her skills as a historian to good effect in this book. And although she acknowledges how angry she has often felt, her biography is not filled with hate. The overall message is one of optimism and faith.

It is a blessing to know Elizabeth and to have shared in her journey. I hope many people read this moving story and benefit from hearing her positive message.

Nancy Tomes
Professor of History

Introduction

I met Elizabeth Brechter about two years ago, when she was a member of one of my classes. I saw a person who was struggling with stammering and fear of failure; she no longer stammers and is confident about her future. This little book tells the story of how she achieved this fortunate change. It tells of a person practically programmed for failure – abusive parents who were convinced she would never succeed; excessive drinking; anger that vented itself on coworkers; severe manic depression. Everything for most of her life pointed to killing herself while driving drunk, committing suicide, or a life spent in mental institutions. Why was not one of these her fate? She encountered many people who made her situation worse, but she met others who cared about her and supported her, whether therapists or ordinary people who befriended her. Her first breakthrough was joining Alcoholics Anonymous, where she met a lifelong friend and other people who encouraged her during her worst experiences. Her decision to pursue a college degree, despite obstacles and fears, enabled her to overcome her sense of failure and gain confidence. Finally, her religious faith, often challenged by hard times, sustained her throughout good and bad periods of her life. I have met students with mental problems throughout my teaching career, but I can honestly say that nobody has had Elizabeth's determination to succeed. She still has difficult times of despair: she has not banished her problems, but definitely knows how to deal with them. Elizabeth's story of survival and perseverance may not be everybody's story, but hopefully it will inspire people about to give up to pursue a goal that may save their lives.

Wilbur R. Miller
Professor of History,
Stony Brook University (SUNY)

Chapter One

I was born in Southside Hospital Bay Shore, Long Island, New York in 1951.

I was born into an alcoholic and violent home. My father, Harry, was problem drinker and my mother, Joan, was mentally ill. My father would go into rages and throw things a lot of the time. My parents were both very ill.

We resided in a house at 98 Division Avenue in Blue Point, New York. My father was working on the Long Island Railroad when I was born, and my mother was a housewife. While I was still a baby, my father became a police officer for the Town of Brookhaven, New York. He drove a police car.

My brother, John, was born in 1953 in the same hospital.

I started kindergarten at the age of six years old. My mother held me back one year from going to kindergarten; why, I do not know. I mostly kept to myself in the class and did not have many friends. I was friendly with one boy in the kindergarten class who lived on the same street where I lived—Division Avenue.

In the kindergarten class, we had dances, and none of the boys in the class ever asked me to dance. This made me feel very rejected and alone. I started getting angry at the male sex at such a young age.

My childhood turned out to be a horror. A very unpleasant incident, which I remember, happened when I was six years old. I was raped by a number of neighborhood boys. They held me down on the ground and stuck sticks up my rectum. I do not remember what happened after that.

At this same age, I started having symptoms of mental illness, such as a lot of nervousness, anxiety, and fear of going to school. I also started developing a fear of the opposite sex. Every time my father drove me to school, I was afraid of walking into the school. I was isolated in school and stayed to myself, but was teased by the other children in my class. I guess that I was just different.

In 1960, the Suffolk County Police Department came into existence and took over the Town of Brookhaven Police. My father was now a Suffolk County Police Officer and still drove a police car. He was working for the Fifth Precinct, in Patchogue. I was about eight or nine years old at that time.

One day during one summer, my father took my mother, brother, and me to a policemen's picnic on Fire Island, New York. We took the ferry over to Fire Island. Other police officers and their families were on the ferry. After we arrived at the picnic area on Fire Island, my father disappeared, and he was gone for the whole picnic. My mother was startled. A lot of people at the picnic wondered where my father was.

After the picnic, my father was seen coming off a boat with another woman, and this woman had just a tiny bikini on. I was terrified, and angry at my father. It was obvious that my father was drunk. My mother, I could see, was also very angry at my father. She was wondering what had happened between my father and this other woman. The other woman's name was Eleanor.

My father, mother, brother, and I got on a ferry to get back to our destination, and when we all got into the car, there was a big argument between my mother and father while my father was driving us home. That was all I could remember about that incident.

I was mentally and physically abused by both of my parents. My parents would both yell at me when I was a child, all the time I was growing up. At times, my mother would run after me with a knife and I would run into the bathroom to get away from her and lock the door behind me. She would try to unlock the bathroom door with the knife and I do not remember what happened after that. Once, my mother threw a knife at me while I was sitting at the kitchen table, and it hit me in my left elbow. My elbow started bleeding, and I do not remember what happened after that. At times, I was strapped by my father and hit with sticks off trees.

I did not get along with my grandmother, Samantha, either; she was not nice to me. She was my father's mother. I am not sure why, but my brother was not abused like I was by my parents or by my grandmother. It could have been because he spoke up for himself to both of my parents and to our grandmother, Samantha. I also believe that my parents and grandmother favored my brother over me.

My Uncle John and Aunt Cindy and my cousins lived in Brooklyn, in an apartment building. One of my little pleasures as a child was when Uncle John and Aunt Cindy would come to visit, and they would bring their three children with them, my first cousins John, Doris, and June. John was five years older than I was, Doris was seven years older, and June was thirteen years older. My brother really enjoyed it, too, when Uncle John and Aunt Cindy and our cousins visited, as we had so much fun screaming, laughing, and running around the house or outside of the house. My Uncle John was my father's brother, and my Aunt Cindy was my mother's sister.

Another good memory I had as a child growing up was when my parents took my brother and me traveling to the New England states, the Southern states, and Mid-Atlantic states. A number of the New England states we visited were Rhode Island, Massachusetts, Vermont, and New Hampshire. Some of the Southern states we visited were Maryland and Virginia. The Mid-Atlantic states that we visited were Delaware, Pennsylvania, and West Virginia.

When my parents took us travelling to other states, we stayed at motels most of the time, and I really enjoyed staying in motels. I thought it was fun. The looks of these motel rooms were very interesting to me, and the motels were so clean and had such clean towels.

My parents even took us to Washington, D.C. a couple of times. I remember we stayed in a beautiful hotel there. While in Washington, D.C., we visited the White House, where the President of the United States lives, and we also visited the Capitol. We also visited other beautiful places, which I cannot remember.

On one hand, I enjoyed travelling to these states and to Washington, D. C., with my parents and my brother, but on the other hand, I had some difficulty. I had trouble urinating, and that was painful. I could not pass my urine because I was not home in a familiar place. Eventually, the urine would come out when my bladder was very full.

Another good memory which I have as a child growing up was Christmastime. Every single Christmas, my brother and I received eleven to twelve gifts underneath the beautiful Christmas tree, which was always set up in the dining room. Every year, the beautiful Christmas tree was real. Every Christmas, it would snow, too. Christmas was a happy time for me. My parents were not that loving to me, emotionally, but they showed their love by buying me all of these gifts for Christmas.

When I was nine years old, I started feeling that I wanted to commit suicide, because the pressures at home and in school were horrible. And the mental and physical abuse with both of my parents continued. I always got down on my knees and prayed.

Also, at this age, I had a pet rabbit in a cage and one day, I knocked it around in the cage and I think that I killed it because it died shortly after that. I did not tell anyone what I had done to the rabbit.

As a child growing up, I was told by my father that I was a failure and would never amount to anything. I was not allowed to make mistakes. At a later time, I was told by both of my parents that I was not capable of going to college someday, even though I had voiced to them that I wanted to do so.

Also at the age of nine, I started stuttering really badly. This caused me a lot of anxiety and stress in school. Every time I had to read in class, I would shake and stutter. Students laughed at me and teased me about it.

I also felt that no boys in school ever looked at me. I was always getting crushes on boys who did not have any interest in me. I had so many crushes on boys and chased after so many of them that my self-esteem was so low at a very young age. I believe that as a child, I started having sexual fantasies about myself and boys who did not want me. My sex and love addiction started when I was so young.

My family was Catholic, and I remember we attended Mass every Sunday. We attended a Catholic church in Blue Point, New York. It was a little white church. And every Sunday, after Mass, my father would drive us home and we would have TV dinners for lunch. I enjoyed the TV dinners.

When I was twelve years old, I started using Vicks Formula 44 with alcohol and codeine in it to relieve my anxiety, as I was suffering really badly and had no one to talk to. I was not expressing my feelings. I was also using over-the-counter drugs to relieve my anxiety. All of these substances were kept in the medicine cabinet in the bathroom at home. When my parents were not looking, I would use them. This use of the Vicks Formula and over-the-counter drugs continued for all the time that I was living at home, and for a long time after I left home.

Also, when I was 12 years old, I started being sexually abused by a family member. This person would touch me inappropriately, and this made me very angry. I tried telling my mother about it, but I guess that she was too ill to do anything about it. This sexual abuse went on for many years.

When I was about fourteen years old, I started having temper tantrums. At the age of fifteen, I started drinking beer that was in our fridge. There was always a lot of beer kept in the fridge. I remember the first time that I drank beer; I could not stop and got very drunk. It was as if something went off in my brain. I felt like I was going to pass out and went into the living room and lay down on the couch. My parents were not home. This beer drinking continued, and I think that my parents were in denial about my beer drinking as they never said anything about it to me.

When I was fifteen years old, I became very attracted to a seventeen-year-old guy who worked at the Carvel Ice Cream shop in Blue Point, the town where I lived. I started writing him letters, but he paid no attention to me. I felt very hurt and angry. I had sexual fantasies about him.

I had a very poor image of the opposite sex at this point in my life, because of the way my father had treated me since I was a child, the rejections of boys in school, and the rejection of the guy at the Carvel Ice Cream shop in Blue Point. I felt that I hated all men already, at the age of fifteen, and felt very afraid of them. I believed that I could not ever have sex with a man because I was afraid that it might be very painful.

I remember walking on the sidewalk in Blue Point one afternoon and thinking to myself, "I hate all men! I hate all men!" Although I believed that I hated all men, I had a huge sex drive and for me, my sex and love addiction was having sexual fantasies about males who were unavailable to me, and chasing after males who were not interested in me or unavailable to me. This disease manifests itself in different ways for different people.

When I was sixteen years old, I became very attracted to my Biology teacher. He was a married man. I wanted to have a sexual relationship with him really badly, and fantasized about it. The fact that I could not have this man made me very angry and I started showing my anger toward him. I knew that he was not interested in me.

I did try confiding in this Biology teacher about what was going on at home with my parents, and he sent me to the guidance counselor at the high school. This guidance counselor sent papers home with me to give to my parents to sign. They were papers about my seeing a school psychologist. My parents were outraged and would not sign the papers. My parents thought that it was shameful for their daughter to be seeing a psychologist for help.

The Biology teacher told me that he had no proof that I was being abused at home or that my parents were fighting. That made me very angry. Why was I so attracted to somebody who had no compassion for me and who did not believe me?

I started having panic attacks at the age of sixteen, and my mental symptoms became much worse. I was experiencing a nervous symptom that is known as the feeling of unreality, or derealization. I felt like everything outside of me was far away, mentally, and I felt that my head was in a bubble. Things outside of me also looked distorted, and I had dimness of vision.

I was just terrified all of the time, but kept attending high school. The anxiety I was having was horrendous and I tried to explain to my parents how I was feeling, but they seemed not to understand. Because of my parents not understanding my anxiety, the pressure at home was horrendous and I had panicky feelings in my throat constantly; while I was at school, I had tremendous anxiety there, too, and panicky feelings in my throat. This was truly a horrible experience for me, having to suffer from so much anxiety and panic at home and in school. I mostly stayed to myself in school and did not mingle with the other students. I was too scared. I also went without eating lunches while in school. I stayed in the girls' room during lunch times, drinking instant breakfast. I was starving myself because of my anxiety and depression.

My parents had no choice but to take me to a psychiatrist in Patchogue, New York. I was evaluated by this psychiatrist, and he was kind to me. He prescribed medication called Thorazine and said that I was going to get well, but I did not get well.

I became sicker, and about eleven days after my seventeenth birthday, I suffered a mental breakdown. I was hallucinating: I saw purple stripes all over my bedroom walls, I heard whispers, and I felt that someone was coming after me to kill me. My whole body became stiff, and I shook all over, and I had such an angry look on my face. I walked with my hands in front of my body. I spent a lot of time in bed and could not eat on my own or shower. My mother had to feed me in bed. I had a lot of trouble moving, and my parents had me at home like this for about twelve days. They did not want to take me a mental hospital because they felt that any hospital for the mentally ill was a disgrace. I do not know why, but they did not take me to a regular hospital, either, not even to an emergency room. They were not contacting my psychiatrist at all. I was just left to lie in bed. I did not know what my parents were thinking. I think that my parents were angry at the psychiatrist who had been treating me, because I ended up getting so ill.

My cousin John and his girlfriend Carrie came over to visit one Sunday and Carrie encouraged both of my parents to take me to a hospital called Suffolk Psychiatric Center on Central State Hospital grounds in Central Islip, New York. My parents decided to take me to this hospital.

The following day, while my father drove me to the hospital with my mother in the front seat of the car, I was hallucinating and sitting in the back seat of the car. I remember my hair being in front of my face. I believed that I was holding a baby in my arms and I was moving my arms back and forth. I was also hearing music.

When we arrived at this hospital on Central Islip State Hospital grounds, my parents walked me into Building L-3. I was evaluated for hours by a psychiatrist and answered the questions the best I could. I was not hallucinating at this time. After the evaluation was over, a nice attendant from Building L-4 came over to me in the waiting room and then walked me over to Building L-4, where I would be staying as a patient. I was given medication, but was not told the name of it. Then, I was put to bed.

I remember that evening, a nice nurse brought me dinner and ice cream. That made me feel better, and after I was done with the ice cream, I was given more. I do not remember what happened after that, but about three days after I was in the hospital, I lost my mind completely, and my psychiatrist at the hospital told my parents that I was gone and he did not think that I was going to come out of this insanity.

My parents were heartbroken and all they could really do was pray and cry. I did come out of this insanity after several days, and I truly believe to this day that my God brought me out of it. As far as my parents were concerned, this was a miracle!

The hospital was not a bad place; I made a lot of friends there and talked to the other patients every day. We had group therapy daily, and met with a psychiatrist daily, too. We played games and made baskets. I had fun there, and the food was excellent. I got a lot better in the hospital, and after one month, I went home. Maybe I should have stayed there longer, because the hospital was a much healthier environment than my home with my parents.

After I came out of the hospital, my mother told me about what had happened in the hospital, about my going insane. I was astonished, but grateful to be sane again.

After I got out of the hospital, I went out on my first date with a friend of my brother's. This man, Ron, was five years older than I was. We went to a diner. Then he asked me out on another date. I was flattered to go out with this man, but afraid, too, of having sex with him. On the second date, he took me to the beach at Smith Point County Park, New York. We were lying on the beach in our bathing suits. He wanted to have sex with me, but I was too afraid, and he became very angry with me, and then he took me home. I did not go out with him again.

The yelling and screaming continued with my parents; they were always arguing with each other, as they had never gotten along. My parents, being both ill, were not capable of taking care of me, obviously. I was in severe mental pain in that environment, and my screaming was so bad. I could not stand the mental pain that I was in. Many times, I ran through the rooms of the house screaming, "I can't take it anymore! I can't take it anymore!" I would fall to the floor screaming, and my mother would grab me by the wrists and shake me and try to get me out of these attacks. At times, my mother would strike me and then my father would take over and start striking me, too.

My brother was very affected by what was going on with my mental anguish. He could not sleep, because many nights, I lay awake sitting up in bed yelling and screaming. My parents did not take me back to the hospital. I was also getting into a lot of arguments with family members such as my cousins, and was hurting people within my whole family! I was very bitter, too.

Although I had had the breakdown, I managed to graduate from high school at the age of eighteen years old and receive my high school diploma. I truly believe that it was God's grace that helped me to accomplish this. The year was 1970.

I was an outpatient at Suffolk Psychiatric Center for years, and my psychiatrist there just kept prescribing medications. I felt very doped up, and I was very bitter and furious at God because of all my suffering.

When I was about eighteen years old, my parents took me to see a private psychiatrist named Doctor Correoso in Islip Terrace who was highly recommended by a next-door neighbor. This psychiatrist took me off all the medicines I was on and had me on one medication called Stelazine. He diagnosed me as having anxiety neurosis and said that I was nearly schizophrenic. I was feeling better, but the mental and physical abuse for me went on with my parents and many times, one or the other of my parents would say to me, "Go back to Central Islip! You will never be any better!"

This psychiatrist told me to look for a job. I found a job in an office in Bayport, New York, and it was near home. My behavior at this job was very irrational; I was always showing my temper and crying. I finally got fired from this job, and my psychiatrist told me to go out and get another job. To this day, I am glad that this psychiatrist pushed me out to work.

One evening, a priest in our church parish closed the door on me and told me that I was hopeless, that he could not deal with my mental illness. My grandmother, Samantha, was very nasty to me, as she could not deal with it either. She also had her own nervous problems. My grandmother tended to favor my brother John over me and I never really have understood why.

At this time in my life, I was still drinking a lot of beer, and many evenings, I would walk the streets drinking bottles of wine, either with friends or by myself, smashing the bottles in the street. I was just really sick! I could not deal with what was going on with my parents at home any longer. I wanted to live by myself now and have my own little home. I wanted to be in peace.

One thing that I do remember was having an adorable dog named Barney. He was a beagle hound and had orange ears like flapjacks. I guess that Barney was a little troublesome, therefore, my mother got rid of him. I believe that I was nineteen when my mother got rid of him. I never forgot about that dog. I really loved him so much. To this day, I still think of that dog.

At the age of nineteen, I found a job in a dry cleaning store, bagging clothes. This job was in Bayport, New York and the boss seemed to be nice at first. I was feeling good about myself because I was working again and following the direction of my psychiatrist.

At this same time, I started dating a man by the name of Jack. He was two years older than I was. He always took me to dark places to make out. I was afraid of having sex with him, too. Even though I was afraid of having sex with him, he wanted to marry me, but we were always arguing. Finally, I stopped seeing him on my own. I could not stand his mother; I just did not like her at all.

At the age of twenty-one, I dated a man, Harry, for six months. He was about six years older than I was, and did not treat me very well. I believed that his main interest in me was sex, and all he wanted to do with me when he took me out was park his car in dark places and make out with me. He never really took me to a restaurant to have coffee or to eat. Still, I could not bear the thought of losing him. One night, we had an argument on the phone and he broke off the relationship. This was not the only argument we had ever had, as we had arguments throughout the whole relationship, and he never told me once that he loved me.

One evening, when my parents were not home, I decided that I was going to get my father's police gun out of my parents' bedroom drawer. I planned to shoot myself in the head. I knew just where my father kept the gun. I could not stand the pain that I was in over breaking up with this boyfriend. When I opened up the drawer in my parents' bedroom where the gun was kept, I found that the gun was not there, and I was surprised. I do not remember what I did after that, as I think I just blacked out!

Chapter Two

I was still employed at the dry cleaning store in Bayport, New York at this point in my life, and it was extremely difficult working with my mental illness, as I suffered from a lot of nervous symptoms. I still bagged clothes all day, and the boss yelled a lot. I worked with other people who were not the nicest people. I continued seeing my psychiatrist in Islip Terrace for medication evaluation and counseling. I used to talk to him a lot about what was going on with my parents at home, but he could not help me. All he could do was listen. I felt like I was in prison in my parents' home. Every time I went out, they would ask me where I was going and every time I came home, they would ask me where I had been. Aside from being struck by my parents, I still had my hair pulled at times by my mother.

My brother now lived in Massachusetts, going to school up there. I really cannot say that I missed him. I resented him because he was attending a university, and I had always wanted to go to college. He did come home at times to visit, and I would talk to him. My brother and I never really got along that well; I guess that he could not deal with my mental illness. And I really could not blame him.

I expressed to both of my parents that I wanted to learn how to drive a car. I was told that I was too nervous to drive; my grandmother also told me that I was too nervous to drive. Despite this negativity, I went ahead and applied to a driving school in Patchogue for driving lessons. I paid for the lessons out of my own money. Every time I had a lesson, the instructor told me that I was doing well. I was actually driving!

After a couple of months, I took my first road test and I passed the test the first time! Both of my parents were surprised that I passed the road test, and my grandmother was surprised, too. I received my New York State driver's license and this opened up doors for me. I bought myself a car as soon as possible out of money that I had saved from working. It was an American Blue Hornet and I was so proud of myself.

I was about twenty-two years old now, and the year was 1973. I drove down to Catholic Charities in Mastic one day and met a nice therapist named Clare. I explained to her the situation at home and she was very sympathetic to my feelings. This therapist told me that I could come back to talk to her again, and if I ran into any real trouble, that I could call her. She gave me her phone number at Catholic Charities.

One day, my mother had a slight car accident in the driveway at home. My father was yelling at the top of his lungs at her, and I started yelling at him. It turned out to be a big, violent argument between my father and me. I hated this man. I hated him for all the things he had said to me in the past and had done to me! I ran upstairs to my bedroom and got my bank book. I ran downstairs and got into my blue Hornet car and started out of the driveway.

I heard my mother screaming, "Elizabeth, come back! Come back!"

I screamed back at her and told her that I was getting out of that house! I was also swearing and cursing!

I sped down to Catholic Charities in Mastic. I ran into the building and spoke to Clare and told her what had happened. She called a landlord in Center Moriches and ended up getting me an apartment in Center Moriches on Main Street.

Clare and I both drove to the apartment house together. It was a white building. We met with the landlord, and he seemed nice. I was so grateful that he was taking me in. He looked at me and said, "I could see that there is trouble. I could see it in your eyes."

I do not remember how my parents found out where I was, but they did come to see me that evening and brought some clothes of mine, and my father brought a radio for me. They kept asking me to come home; I refused to come home. I was not going back to that hellhole. That evening, I remember going across the street to the supermarket to buy myself some eggs, bacon, and prune juice.

Clare and I kept in touch, and she always came to visit me. I had to apply for Social Services because I had no job; I had decided not to go back to my job at the dry cleaners because the boss was always yelling. But dealing with Social Services was a nightmare. This experience caused me a lot of stress. I had to stand in a long line in order to receive an application. On the application, I had to answer a lot of personal questions, and I was truly at my wit's end. I waited about a month before I got any financial help from Social Services; Catholic Charities helped me out in the meantime.

At this point in my life, I started attending Doctor Abraham Low's Recovery Program, which was called Recovery Incorporated. At the Recovery meetings, the people who attended and I would read from Doctor Low's book, *Mental Health Through Will-Training,* and then give examples about situations that occurred during the past week or present week, and how we controlled our tempers. At these meetings, we were taught spotting techniques or slogans to help us to control our tempers.

I worked at an auto parts place for about six months, doing bookkeeping, and my behavior was very irrational, but the boss did not ever fire me. He felt sorry for me, and he and I became good friends.

I eventually went into a rehabilitation-training program at a center in Oakdale. It was a day program for the mentally and physically disabled. Clare and an occupational vocational rehabilitation counselor at an agency in Hauppauge, New York got me into this program.

At first, I liked attending the training. I spent my days doing office work within the program. I did enjoy this. While I was attending this program, I met up with a guy by the name of John. He was about five years younger than I was and I was very attracted to him. He had curly blond hair and brown eyes. He was also very tall. We dated for about six months, but it was a very unhealthy relationship. We were always arguing. This guy was not a drinker, but I continued to drink alcohol at times, and was still using cough medicine a lot of the time to relieve my anxiety.

My behavior at this program was not good all of the time; I was irrational sometimes, and the counselors would speak to me. I knew that there was something wrong with me. I now attended Catholic Charities and saw the psychiatrist regularly, and also saw my therapist Clare. I took medication, but the medication could not control my behavior.

At home, I remember throwing things at the apartment wall at times, as I was a very angry and raging person, like both of my parents. I may as well say that I was a violent person at times and I was always losing my temper. I did not realize it at the time, but the alcohol and abuse of cough medicine with alcohol and codeine in it was really taking a toll on my life. I was always thinking about suicide and spoke a lot about it to people, but no one called the police on me at this point in my life.

In about one year, I got transferred to the rehabilitation-training program in Riverhead and continued doing office work. I met up with another guy there, also named John. We had a six-month relationship. We lived together at my new apartment in Riverhead. I did not enjoy having sex with this man, as I did not trust him. It was a violent relationship; we both drank and he was also using drugs. We also both had mental illness. In a drunken rage, I struck him one day; we got into a big physical fight, and I had cuts on my body.

Eventually, he left; I told him to get out, and he harassed me for months. I had to go to the Riverhead Police Dept. for help; he was arrested a couple of times for harassing me, and I spent days in court over this issue. Finally, he was committed to Central Islip State Hospital for the harassment.

After all this occurred, I was appointed to a job at Family Court in Hauppauge New York as a clerk typist. The year was 1976 and I was about twenty-five years old. I was terrified to go to work on the first day. The first day of work was always hard for me. I was working in the petition office with many other young women, typing out petitions, and I was being trained by someone who was not that patient with my mistakes. I was extremely nervous every day because of my mental illness. I finally was taken off this job and sent to work in the file room downstairs. I was extremely upset about that. I felt like a failure, but continued going to work every day.

I moved to Centerport, New York at this time in my life and was living in an upstairs apartment in an old house. As time went on, I did not get along with the other tenants so well, because of my anger; I also had mood swings every day of my life. Either I was very, very happy or very, very depressed. Depression continued to be a big part of my life, along with suicidal thinking, and I would always discuss my suicidal thoughts with people. I was always calling the Response of Suffolk County Hotline for help, and I spoke to the hotline counselors all of the time.

I continued to work at Family Court. My behavior at my job was very irrational at times; I would show my temper at work and had great difficulty getting along with the staff. Working with mental illness, obviously, was very hard for me. I was going from one mental health center to another at this point in my life, just speaking with therapists, seeing psychiatrists, and refusing medications. I was ignorant and did not want to be on any medication. I was still drinking alcohol and using cough medicine, and also got addicted to prescription drugs at this point in my life.

In 1978, I started attending Suffolk County Community College in Selden, New York, because I wanted to fulfill my dream. I always wanted to go to college and wanted to prove to myself that I was not the failure that my parents said I was. I chose Accounting as my major. I would sit up at nights studying and using cough medicine and the prescription drugs and still drinking alcohol at times. That helped me cope with the stresses of work and school and somehow, I did so well in school! I was finding out that I was intelligent, after all.

My parents had moved down to Florida. I can't say that I missed them. I did not miss the aggravation. Every time that I saw them in the past, they were always criticizing me and telling me what to do. I just could not cope with them.

I continued working at Family Court for years, and still could not get along with co-workers. Many times, I got into real bad arguments with co-workers. It got to the point where I was spoken to by one of the bosses. Although my job was permanent, I was in danger of getting fired in the future because of my sick behavior. I was very worried, but then again, I was pointing the finger at everybody else and was failing to look at myself. I still was furious at God, ever since my first mental breakdown in 1968. I blamed God for my miserable life.

While I worked at Family Court, over the years, I moved to a couple of different places. When I left my job there in 1980, I moved to Coram, New York. I rented out a room from a really nice woman and her husband; she seemed to have a lot of compassion for what I had gone through, with my past and with my parents.

I was now working for a company in Commack, New York as an inventory clerk. Again, I had trouble dealing with co-workers. One of the workers saw that there was something terribly wrong with me, mentally, and she started harassing me. That was really hard for me to deal with. And at this point in my life, I was having serious menstrual problems and had to be hospitalized for a D&C scraping of the uterus. This was a very scary experience for me. I was also back and forth to different gynecologists because of an on-going vaginal infection. I was always in a lot of pain over that. I could no longer take the antibiotics vaginally because I was allergic to all of them that the doctors tried on me. Finally, I met up with a woman who had the same problem I did; she told me to keep inserting yogurt up my vaginal area a couple of times of day, and that helped. And although I had had the D&C scraping, the irregular menstrual periods still continued. This was a rough thing for me to live with. Vaginal examinations were very hard for me, as they were very painful. The doctors who examined me did not understand my nervousness. I was getting very bitter toward these doctors.

Within six months, I got fired from that job in Commack because of my mental and physical problems. I had to deal with Suffolk County Dept. of Social Services again and believe me, it was not easy. It meant standing in long lines to get an application. I also had to deal with the New York State Department of Labor to apply for unemployment insurance. Finally, I was given the unemployment; I also received food stamps from Department of Social Services (DSS).

I had moved out to Holbrook at this point in my life. I liked the room I was living in, in a house at first, and became friendly with the tenant who was living in the house and her husband. They had about three children altogether. The landlord seemed to be nice at first. I ended up falling in lust with a mechanic who worked at an auto service center down the block. He did not have any interest in me, and that made me very angry. All of my life, I did have a habit of running after unavailable men. Maybe I was getting some kind of a high out of hurting myself.

I started writing letters and making inappropriate phone calls to where the mechanic worked! I even sent pornographic pictures to this service center and finally, they called up my parents, who were living on Long Island again, not too far from where I lived. The mechanics explained to my parents what I was doing, and my parents yelled at me for it. I stopped bothering the mechanic at that auto service center.

In time, the next-door tenants and I became enemies, as I was complaining about their children playing, because of all the noise that they were making. There was arguing. I was still attending Suffolk County Community College at this time, still drinking, and still using cough medicine and pills. I attended a mental health clinic in Holbrook, New York, seeing a psychiatrist and a therapist, but it did not seem to help my mental illness. I was a crazy woman and my temper was out of control. I was still not on any medications. As time went on, my life just became progressively worse, and the born-again Christians from a church down the street started coming to my door all the time to bring me to their church. They knew that I was a miserable woman. But all I did was yell at them.

Chapter Three

In 1981, I moved to an apartment in West Babylon and got another job at a manufacturing company in Lindenhurst, New York. I worked in an office, in a factory now, as an inspector. The company manufactured airplane parts, and my job was to inspect the airplane parts. I was doing a good job, but then again, I had trouble coping with co-workers and found it hard to get along with a lot of the women there. And the men in the factory made sexual overtures to me and I found that very hard to deal with. My anxiety, which I suffered from on a daily basis, was sky high at this point. The bosses even made sexual overtures to me. I let it be known that I did not approve of that. I worked on this job for about a year and then got fired. There was absolutely nothing I could do about that. I just picked myself up, like I always did, and moved on.

After about six months, I got a job at a manufacturing company in Hauppauge, New York, another job as an inspector. I do not remember what I inspected, but it was the same story: I struggled with co-workers, my behavior was very irrational at times, and a lot of times, I was reprimanded for my behavior by my immediate boss. Again, I was pointing the fingers at everybody else! At this time in my life, I do remember that there was a lot of drunk driving in my story. I would get behind the wheel of my car so intoxicated, and I thank God that I did not end up killing somebody else down the road.

Because of my irrational behavior at this job, I was teased or harassed by men in the factory, and women who worked there shied away from me. I was a loner on the job.

Finally, it got to the point, in 1983, when I was about thirty-two years old, I tried going back to church and became born-again and was having a relationship with Jesus Christ. I then became fanatical and tried to push my beliefs on my co-workers, and that just caused me more problems at my job. I hated my job and I hated going into work there every day, and my mood swings were so bad! Again, I was either very happy or very depressed, and my co-workers knew that there was something badly wrong with me. I was just in a lot of denial.

While I was still working at this job, a lady came into my life who later became the best friend I ever had. Her name was Sarah. I met her at a women's group at a therapist's home in Sayville, New York. Sarah told me that I could call her every day and we started to get to know one another. She was a lovely woman, and she was about nineteen years older than I was. She had so much intelligence and wisdom.

It was obvious to her that I was a miserable person. Yes, I was miserable—I hated the world and I hated myself. And I was constantly pointing the finger at everyone else. Sarah brought to my attention, one day, that even though I had gotten a lot of treatment all of my life, I did not seem to be making progress at this point and that I was such an unhappy person. She suggested I go to Alcoholics Anonymous.

I didn't quite understand why she was telling me to go to Alcoholics Anonymous. And I said to her, "Why should I go to AA? I am not an alcoholic!" I had never had one social drink, since I started drinking cough medicine at the age of twelve and beer at the age of fifteen, but every time I drank, I drank to get drunk.

Sarah took me, alcoholic or not, to my first AA meeting one evening in 1984 at a Lutheran church in Islip Terrace. I was living in a cottage in East Islip by now. When I walked into an upstairs room in the church, everyone was laughing and smiling before the meeting started, and I wondered why they were so happy. I thought to myself, "Why are they so happy? They are alcoholics."

I really enjoyed the meeting that evening; someone was celebrating his anniversary in AA, but I forget how many years. They served cake and coffee, and I loved that, although I really felt that I did not belong there. I remember that a man sat in the front of the room and spoke about his experience, strength, and hope. Everybody was laughing. I enjoyed the meeting, but did not intend to go back.

I attended a Catholic church in East Islip, New York at this time in my life. There was a young priest who served Mass there, whom I was very attracted to. I wrote letters to him and made phone calls. It was obvious that he did not want me and that made me angry. I was a manipulator and I actually had thought that I could take this man away from the priesthood!

One day, the pastor of that church and I had a big argument out in the parking lot by the church. He was just sick and tired of my disgusting behavior. He told me that I had a problem, and I told him that I did not have a problem! I was very upset by this argument and continued on my way, suffering mentally. The only one who really had any compassion for me was Sarah. I talked to her about everything.

Six months after Sarah took me to my first meeting of Alcoholics Anonymous, I went to a meeting one evening on my own, in Central Islip, New York. It was June of 1985. I think that it was an Open Discussion meeting. Prior to this, I begged God for mercy. I told God that I could not stand the mental pain any longer, and if I was not directed to some kind of help, I was going to end it all! Sarah continued to tell me to go to AA.

At this meeting, I identified with the speaker. He was talking about his childhood and how bad his childhood was. It brought me back to my childhood, but I still did not believe that I was an alcoholic, or maybe I just was not ready to admit it.

From this evening on, I just kept attending the Open Meetings and Open Discussion Meetings of AA. The people were very nice to me and kept saying to me, "Keep coming back, Liz. You are in the right place." During coffee breaks, all I did was talk about my past drunks to these people, and I kept looking over the steps and the traditions.

I was still showing up for my job, even though I was so miserable there, and I was still attending Suffolk County Community College and doing well there! But it got to the point at my job that I was being fired, and the boss gave me time to find another job. And I was having difficulty finding another job. I really felt that I was under such pressure at my job and I could not get along with anyone there. I had mentioned to my boss and co-workers that I was attending AA now, and the response that I got was, "You're not an alcoholic!"

I kept talking to Sarah on a daily basis, and all she could do was listen, but listening to her was very soothing. After attending the AA Open Meetings and Open Discussion Meetings for about three and a half months, I wanted to drive my car into a pole one day or go to a liquor store, because I was being fired from my job. I stayed sober by attending the Open Meetings and Open Discussion Meetings.

My Sobriety Date was July 26, 1985. I did not go to the liquor store that day. I kept on driving home, and in the car, I talked to God and admitted to God that I had a problem with alcohol. I took the first step of Alcoholics Anonymous in the car.

"I admit I am powerless over alcohol and that my life has become unmanageable."

I was relieved. I finally got home and called the AA Hotline and talked to a nice lady on the phone who was another recovering alcoholic. She told me to get to a meeting that evening. Sarah was very happy about me admitting to myself that I was an alcoholic.

I did go to a meeting that evening, but did not share that I was an alcoholic. However, I kept going back to AA. Soon, I joined a group at a church in Islip and I got a sponsor. I got into the steps and I was now officially a member of AA! I was so happy and people in AA were saying to me, "Congratulations!"

AA was home to me, but as time went on, a lot of anger and rage was coming out of my mouth. I had a lot of pain from my childhood and apparently, I had difficulty expressing a lot of my feelings over the past years of my life. I kept losing sponsors because they could not handle my anger and rage. I was still getting professional help, but it was not helping the anger and rage. People in AA who could stick by me and support me were really supporting me, and those people were saving my life. AA saved my life.

I truly believe that if I had not gotten into AA when I did, that I would probably have died young; I was only thirty-three years old.

I had to stop attending Suffolk County Community College at this point because it was too much for me to handle along with all the meetings I was going to. I had become very dedicated to the AA Program of Recovery. I had so much anger and rage inside of me, and when I shared, at just about every meeting, I would yell and sometimes run out of the room. People at the meetings would run after me and talk to me and try to calm me down. Because I was losing so many sponsors, a woman in AA suggested a sponsorship group for me. My anger was too great for any one person to handle. So, three women got together and sponsored me, and it worked out.

In my early sobriety, I was trying to make amends to people I had harmed while I was out there drinking. This was very dangerous. If people did not accept my amends, I could have started drinking over it. I did make amends to certain people I had harmed in the past, and some of them accepted my apologies. Other people did not; I did go to that Catholic priest whom I had harmed with all of the letters and phone calls. He was not receptive to my apologies, and that hurt me a great deal. I had called or written to people within my biological family and tried to make amends to them, and some of my cousins forgave me for mean things I had said to them in the past and were glad that I was now a member of Alcoholics Anonymous!

I tried to tell my parents that I was an alcoholic, but they did not believe me. They said that they did not ever see me drunk.

After my brother started attending a university in Massachusetts, he stayed there and never came back. He was about thirty-one years old now, but every time I spoke to him, I tried to tell him about my being an alcoholic and he said that I was crazy! He did not believe that I was an alcoholic, either.

It was denial on my family's part. They just could not believe it, probably because they had their own problems. I really considered AA my family now, too. The people in AA loved me and were really trying to save my life.

My relationship with God was changing; I loved God a lot more now. I was, for the first time in my life, developing a real relationship with God. I really prayed on a daily basis. I had been taught, years ago, that God was an angry and punishing God. Now, through AA, I knew that my God was a loving and merciful God. I did not believe in Hell any longer. I developed a completely different perception of God. I felt that, within my life, I had already been to Hell! I also knew that I was lucky to be alive. I continued to attend the Catholic Church because it was the church of my birth.

Chapter Four

One of the ladies who sponsored me was an alcoholism counselor, and when I was about nine months sober, she suggested that I start attending ACOA Workshops at South Oaks Hospital in Amityville, New York. ACOA stands for Adult Children of Alcoholics. South Oaks was a private psychiatric hospital, and these workshops ran on Saturdays over at the facility. I did attend these workshops religiously, every Saturday. They were very hard for me to handle. Other people in the groups talked constantly about their childhoods, and there was a lot of crying going on in the groups, and I was very upset all of the time and crying about my own childhood. I had a really hard time talking about my childhood and how I suffered. Maybe I was not ready to attend ACOA at that time. It was obvious to other people in the groups that I had a lot of rage and anger. That made it very uncomfortable for other people in the groups.

I did celebrate one year of sobriety, in July of 1986, with my group at the time, which was at a Catholic church in Bay Shore. One hundred people showed up at that anniversary! I was attending so many different groups at that point in my sobriety and knew so many people that it was such a beautiful anniversary; of course, my parents were not there. My parents could not face the fact that I was an alcoholic in recovery, as they had their own diseases that they could not face. I was dressed up really nicely, and my hair looked beautiful, and I had two female speakers.

I found my second year of sobriety to be harder than the first. In the meantime, I had taken a civil service test for Suffolk County. The position was clerk-typist, and I ended up getting a very high mark on the test and got appointed to a civil service job at the Suffolk County Dept. of Social Services.

I first worked in an office in Amityville, New York and this job I enjoyed at first, but the job turned out to be extremely stressful. The phone work was very hard; I had to deal with very angry clients on the phone, and I had enough anger of my own. I was also having some problems dealing with some co-workers, as I took everything so personally. Finally, this particular office moved to a Bay Shore location and I continued working for the agency. The stress and anxiety that I experienced was horrendous. However, I got a lot of support from the women in AA.

I was also attending Overeaters Anonymous meetings at this point in my recovery, because of my bingeing on food. Many nights, I sat up bingeing on all different kinds of food. I was trying to fill that emptiness inside of me, and I was very lonely for a man. With all of the problems I had with my anger, I really expected to have a healthy relationship with a man?

I lived in an apartment in a private house in East Islip, New York. I had to move out of my cottage in East Islip because I was having problems with the landlady and her family; they made a lot of noise outside of their house, and I kept complaining to them. Finally, I was asked to leave. My history with living in apartments was not good, as I did not have positive experiences. I was very sensitive to noise.

Although I continued to work in my AA program and was into the steps and calling my sponsor daily, the pressures at work really built up. I felt that I could not tolerate the pressure any longer and felt that I was headed for a nervous breakdown! I also still attended the ACOA workshops, too.

I knew that I needed further help, but was not sure of what kind of help to seek. I was two and a half years sober now, but was at the end of my rope and bingeing on food.

One morning, in January of 1988, I woke up in a horrendous depression; I felt that I was losing control of my mind. I called South Oaks Hospital for help and asked the lady on the phone in Administration if I could admit myself into the hospital that day. I explained to her how I was feeling. She said that I could. I called up a woman friend in AA and asked if she and her husband could take me to South Oaks Hospital, as I was signing myself in. She said that she and her husband would be able to take me. That day, they drove me to Valentine Hall, which was where Admitting was located.

A psychiatrist asked me a whole bunch of questions, and one of the questions he asked was, "Do you want to commit suicide?"

I kept saying "No."

And I meant it. I felt severely depressed, as I felt that I did not have any energy at all in me and did not feel like doing anything. But, I did not want to kill myself at this point, and I truly believed that I did not want to die.

He did not seem like he believed me. Later on, I was taken upstairs in Valentine Hall to a locked psychiatric unit. It was horrible being in a psychiatric hospital again, especially a locked unit. I just wished that I had never gone there, but I knew that I had to be there. I felt that I was losing my mind again. I did call a co-worker at my job at DSS and let her know where I was.

I was now thirty-six years old.

I ended up being on suicide watch for about one week. It was horrible. Nurses kept looking at me through a little window. It was very humiliating. There was no group therapy in this unit—only occupational therapy. I did walk around the unit, and day by day, I felt better. The food was good in this hospital. I watched some television. They kept nagging me about taking medication, but I refused. I did not want to be on any tranquilizers. I had a long history of abusing prescription drugs.

I talked on the pay phone to people in AA and also contacted people in the AA Recovery Program. I also called my parents, who had moved down to Florida again; my mother was very upset that I was in a psychiatric hospital! I tried to explain to her that I needed to be there, as I needed help, but she did not understand.

After one week, I went to a locked unit downstairs in Valentine Hall—in this unit, I participated in group therapy led by a social worker, and we had a lot of activities, like going over to the gym. I really did not enjoy myself at all, but was glad that I got myself to the hospital. My psychiatrist in the hospital sat down with me one day and explained to me that my depression was nothing to be ignored and that it could cause me to drink again someday. I had clinical depression, he said, and I also suffered from severe pre-menstrual syndrome. He said that lithium could help me. Finally, I consented to taking medication. I agreed to take the lithium, and was happy about taking it.

I asked my psychiatrist what my diagnosis was.

He said, "Chronic mental illness," and he also told me that I had suffered a breakdown.

After about three weeks, I was transferred into the Eating Disorder Unit and was diagnosed as having anorexia and bulimia. Bulimia is abnormal hunger, and in my case, I binged on food all of the time. I had an eating disorder and I was being treated for it now. I was proud of myself for that. So, I really made a good choice by signing myself into the hospital, and my insurance paid for the treatment.

I started all my hard work in the Eating Disorder Unit—I had primary groups every morning where I talked about my childhood, and it was not easy. I ended up dealing with my childhood abuse issues and the sexual abuse issues of the past. I jumped up and down and I screamed and I yelled. A lot of anger was coming out of me. I also dealt with the issue over the rabbit that I possibly killed when I was nine years old, because I felt horrible about what I had done to the rabbit. When I spoke about what I had done to the rabbit, I was hysterical crying and kept saying, "I hope the rabbit forgives me." The counselors would say to me, "The rabbit forgives you."

I even had Family Sculpture therapy in the hospital. This had to do with someone playing my mother, someone played my father, grandmother, etc., and the therapy was very loud. A lot of anger surfaced.

I also attended Overeaters Anonymous meetings in the hospital.

I left the hospital after about two months, in March, 1988, and went home to my apartment in East Islip. I was definitely better, but all my problems were not over. I still had to deal with life on life's terms. After several weeks, I went back to my job at DSS. That was not a good choice. My psychiatrist at South Oaks did not want me going back there, but I felt I needed the money.

Chapter Five

After I returned to my job at DSS, I continued to have problems with co-workers and with supervisors. My anxiety level was very high, but I continued taking my lithium on a daily basis. It really did not seem to help me, or, maybe I was overriding the medication, as the job was extremely stressful for me.

I still saw my psychiatrist at South Oaks Outpatient department once a week. At some later point, I did start to see a psychiatrist at Stony Brook University Hospital, because I still suffered from depression and felt that I needed to try another doctor and get another opinion. I was diagnosed as having manic-depressive disorder by this second psychiatrist, and she kept me on lithium and told me to increase the medication during my menstrual periods. That worked well for me. I also moved out to Patchogue, New York, in 1989. I had a small apartment, and I got my first cat. I named the cat Charlie and loved him to pieces.

In 1989, also, my brother got married. I did not attend his wedding, because I felt that I could not handle all of the drinking at the wedding. My brother held a resentment toward me for a long time because of that. My brother and I had a pretty up-and-down relationship all of our lives. It was never a working relationship.

In 1990, I returned to Suffolk County Community College. I felt ready to go back, mentally, and had achieved five years of sobriety, at this point. It was not easy going back to college; I had to get use to studying again and doing assignments. But despite all of the struggles I was having, I was doing it.

As time went on, the situation at my job got worse with co-workers and supervisors. In 1991, I resigned from my job at DSS. I also checked into Stony Brook University Hospital to have a total hysterectomy operation, because of irregular menstrual periods and bleeding in between periods. After the surgery, I was told that I also had endometriosis, which is a disease of the uterus. And during my life, I had suffered much with this disease.

My parents had moved back to New York at this time in my life. They had lived down in Florida for years, but now bought a little gray house in Patchogue not far from where I lived. After my surgery, my mother and father helped me out a lot with food shopping, and my mother did my laundry. They were a big help to me, and I don't know what I would have done without them. I just could never have a healthy ongoing relationship with them, because neither of them had ever gone for professional help. That was very sad.

In this same year, in June, I graduated from Suffolk County Community College, Selden, New York with an Associate's Degree in Applied Science. Both of my parents were at the ceremony. It was a very long event. I wore a white cap and gown, and my father apologized to me for calling me a failure in the past.

I suffered with my back on and off, too, as I had had back problems for many years and had gone for chiropractic treatment at different times in my life. Even though I had chronic problems with my back, I remember working for the cattery at an animal shelter in Riverhead, New York for a number of years. During my employment at this animal shelter, I adopted quite a number of cats. I also moved to another apartment in Patchogue, on River Avenue. At first, I was happy with this apartment. It had three large rooms, and the landlady seemed to be nice.

I ended up getting fired from my job at the animal shelter. After that, I had a series of other jobs that did not last, and I had to go to DSS for help many times. Finally, in 1994, I got onto Social Security Disability. DSS helped me to get onto it. After I got onto SSD, I started working part-time because of my mental illness.

I still attended Alcoholics Anonymous religiously; I had never left the program. Somewhere along the line, I also started attending the Al-Anon Recovery Program, because of the alcoholism throughout my whole family. I had had an uncle who died from alcoholism a long time ago. Aside from attending AA, the Al-Anon Recovery Program helped me a lot. AA was to keep me sober and Al-Anon was teaching me how to live as a sober person. I felt that I needed both programs. I was also still attending Overeaters Meetings at this time of my life, to help me keep my anorexia under control. I was very dedicated to all of my programs.

My father died in November, 1994 from emphysema; he smoked cigarettes for sixty years of his life. This was very sad for me and my whole family. Even though my father hurt me so badly in the past, I was devastated when he died. I could not stop crying at meetings and I kept sharing about my father. A lot of people from AA and Al-Anon came to the wake and the funeral. I missed my father so badly and really believed that the pain would never go away. My father was buried in Calverton National Cemetery, Calverton, New York.

After his death, I started attending a bereavement group in Brookhaven, New York; it helped me to be around other people who had had the same kind of loss. My mother took my father's death very badly, and my brother told me that our father was a good dad, and I agreed with him.

After my father died, I worked at a veterinarian hospital in West Sayville as a kennel person. It was very hard for me to go to work at this job daily, even though it was part-time, because the grieving over my father's death was so heavy. I eventually ended up getting fired from that job because I had trouble getting along with co-workers. I collected my unemployment benefits and food stamps.

I knew that because of my mental illness, I had such difficulty at jobs getting along with co-workers and staff. But I never gave up working—I just kept trying, hoping that someday, things would get better. I also went from one psychiatrist to another, and getting a lot of therapy from social workers who worked at different agencies. I lived in hope that some day, I would find a psychiatrist and a therapist whom I would really like and get along with. I never stopped taking my medications.

In 1994, also, I went onto the Section 8 HUD program and had to move again, because Section 8 did not approve of my apartment on River Avenue in Patchogue. HUD stands for Housing and Urban Development, which is a federally funded program that pays part of tenants' rents. The tenants on this program pay the part of their rent that HUD does not pay. The part of the rent that the tenants on HUD do not pay is called the rent subsidy.

The apartment that I lived in on River Avenue, Patchogue, had no kitchen facilities, such as a fridge or a stove, and it did not meet all the requirements of the program. I then found an apartment on Main Street, Patchogue. This was a one-bedroom apartment; I lived there with all of my cats. But Charlie had died. I had to have him put to sleep because one day, he just went violent; I missed him so badly.

In 1995, I starting seeing a naturopathic physician, as she was associated with the New York State Association of Naturopathic Physicians. Her name was Doctor Ashley Lewin, and I saw her for my food issues and other issues, such as Candida, which is a yeast infection throughout the whole body. I had had vaginal infections all of my life, and believed that it was Candida. I also felt tired all of the time. Doctor Lewin and I started on a journey together, and she later became very instrumental in my mental health recovery.

In 1996, I got a job as a housekeeper at a department store in Patchogue. I really enjoyed this job at first. I liked what I was doing, and I had a really nice supervisor. I had to work with three other housekeepers, and I did not find that to be easy. But, I really enjoyed going to this job daily, and, it was part-time. As time went on, I had some real problems with the other housekeepers, but was handling it.

About a year after I was hired at this department store, my mother moved up to Massachusetts to be close to my brother and his family. One morning, she had surgery, for an obstruction in her bowels, and never came out of the surgery. I remember my brother calling me the next morning after her surgery, and telling me that she had died! I was shocked and couldn't believe that my mother, the woman who gave me life, was gone! Even though my mother had hurt me so badly in the past, I still felt a horrible emptiness on the inside. My brother was crying so badly.

I went to work that morning; it was hard for me to function as a housekeeper, but I was functioning and using the tools of Doctor Low's Recovery Program. One of Doctor Low's slogans is, "Don't tell me how you feel. Tell me if you are functioning."

A few days later, my mother's wake was held at the same funeral home in Patchogue, New York where my father's wake had been held. Her funeral was at the same church, and a lot of people from AA and Al-Anon Programs came to both the wake and the funeral. It was so sad! I could not cry at all. When my dad died, I cried a lot. My mother was then laid to rest in the same cemetery as my father, in the same grave.

I did not cry over my mom's death for months. I did attend a bereavement group again and it helped.

And life went on.

Chapter Six

In 1999, when I was fourteen years sober, I still worked at the department store as a housekeeper. Also, I started dating a man in AA named Tim. He had trouble staying sober, and little did I know that I had made a bad choice. I liked him a lot and I was attracted to him. I just wanted a man in my life so badly, because I truly felt that another person was going to made me happy. This relationship was not healthy; we argued all of the time. Tim did not drive, as he had lost his driver's license due to drinking and driving.

I was seeing a therapist at this time at her home in East Patchogue; we talked a lot about this man during our sessions. She told me that I was not to break off with this man without her permission. I did think to myself, "Who is she to tell me what to do? I am the one who is suffering with all this anxiety in this relationship."

This therapist also taught me how to do some inner child work by holding my right hand over my heart and speaking lovingly to my inner child. My inner child was very wounded and needed a lot of healing. I used this technique that she taught me daily.

Because of Tim's relapsing, he did go into a program at Pilgrim State Hospital where he had to live for a while in a certain building over there. This was a transitional services program for people who were having difficulty with their recovery. Tim would call me from a phone booth, or I would call him. We were not getting along very well and at times, he would get nasty with me. I just felt that I could not handle being involved with him any longer and I really felt that I needed someone whom I could marry someday. Finally, one day, when Tim called me, I broke off the relationship with him and I felt relieved. I was not suffering much at all over this breakup. I did see my therapist afterward and told her that I had broken off with Tim and she accepted it, as she did not say anything negative to me.

I ended up leaving this therapist because I really was not that happy with her. I saw a few therapists after her. As far as my job at the department store went, I ended up quitting that job because of chronic back pain. I just could not do the heavy housekeeping anymore, and I could not give any notice because I was in so much pain with my lower back. As time went on, the pain in my lower back, and even in my legs, got worse. I remember doing some volunteer work for a while, because I was not one to be without work.

In 2002, I got a volunteer job at a mental health agency in Patchogue as a junior companion to the mentally ill. The name of this mental health agency was the Federation of Organizations. I really liked this job, even though my back was hurting me so badly on a daily basis. Some of my duties were to make breakfast for the clients, lead groups for the clients, and do paperwork. I worked in the Day Social Program from about eight o'clock in the morning until two o'clock in the afternoon. Eventually, I went out to different adult homes through this agency, visited with the mentally ill in these adult homes, and led groups. I liked the work.

One day, I sat down at a table in the Day Social Program alongside this elderly lady who was a client there. She had the cutest face, with a fat nose and big ears, and I found out that she was Italian. I am half-Italian. Her name was Carmella and I fell in love with her right away. From then on, we became friends. I was sitting at a table with her daily in the program. She used to yell at me at times.

While I worked at this mental health agency, I dated a guy by the name of Mark for about six months. All he ever did was talk about his past to me, and I had a lot of trouble dealing with this. I was attracted to him, but really did not love him. It got to the point where we were engaged, but because we could not get along, one day he called me and we argued and he broke off the relationship. I was very upset. I really thought that I was going to marry this man! I was so upset that I called a friend and mentioned to her that I was in a lot of pain over this relationship break-up and wanted to take pills and end it all!

I later heard a knock on my door. It was the Suffolk County Police – Fifth Precinct! I tried to tell these two police officers that I was all right and was not going to harm myself, but one of the officers insisted that I take a ride with them. He told me that they had to take me up to Stony Brook University Hospital Psychiatric Emergency Services for a psychiatric evaluation. I was not too happy about that, but went with them without any struggle.

The officers were very nice to me and did not handcuff me. Usually, people are handcuffed when being taken to Stony Brook University Hospital Psychiatric Emergency Services. On the way there, the officer who was driving the police car kept talking to me, to help me to calm down, and I liked him a lot. He seemed like such a nice man. I'd say that he was in his forties. After we arrived at CPEP, as the Comprehensive Psychiatric Emergency Program was called, I found that it was a locked unit. And that was so scary to me. I could not have any water, and I had to take off my shoes and socks and put on the unit's socks, and my pocketbook was taken away from me.

I must have waited in the waiting area, with the police officers watching me, for about two hours to see a doctor. After I went into a room to see a doctor, the police officers left me. I was terrified of being admitted into the hospital! The doctor was very nice and asked me questions about my past, including my childhood. Then he asked me why I said that I wanted to commit suicide, and I explained to him why and kept trying to reassure him that I did not mean to say that, and that I was feeling much better now. The doctor let me go home. I was so relieved and knew that I did not ever want to go back there again. It was such a frightening experience. That evening, upon leaving the hospital, I went home by taxi.

I went through the grieving process of losing a boyfriend and just talking about it to the women in my program support system. As time went on, the pain got easier. I knew that I was better off without this man. It was not a healthy relationship. I continued doing my volunteer work at the Federation in Patchogue, and kept talking to Carmella at the table; my love for this little Italian lady was growing and growing. I really understood her mental illness and as time went on, we became close friends. After programs every day, I would help her up into the bus that took her to her adult home.

My back did not get any better. The pain kept getting worse. Finally, I went to see a neurosurgeon in East Patchogue. X-rays were taken of my lower back. This doctor told me that I definitely needed spinal fusion surgery. I was so scared. He explained to me that I had a hanging disk at the bottom of my spine, and the surgeon had to remove the disk, then put a bone in in its place, and then screws to hold the bone in. He also told me that I would be wearing a big back brace for about six weeks after the surgery.

Chapter Seven

In June of 2003, I went to Brookhaven Memorial Hospital in Patchogue to have spinal fusion surgery. Before the surgery, on the operating table, I was crying. I was so afraid. But before I knew it, I was out like a light. The next thing I remember was waking up in the recovery room. The pain was not all that bad. I was lying on my stomach and knew that I had an incision in my back.

Both of my parents were deceased, so they could not come to see me in the hospital. People from AA came to see me, and also staff from the Federation, where I worked, came to see me. That gave me a lot of joy. I had quite a lot of visitors.

I was told, before the surgery, that I was going to need a walker when getting out of bed the first time. Needless to say, I was so determined to walk without a walker and I kept telling myself that I could do it! I also prayed to my God for help to walk on my own and sure enough, I got up out of bed on my own. I was so proud of myself and the staff on the ward was amazed with me. My doctor, who operated on my spine, came to see me in the hospital and I was so happy to see him. I went home in four days only, because I was so determined to keep on walking.

I was fitted for a back brace and before I knew it, I had the brace and wore it outside of my clothes. Although I had spinal fusion surgery, I went back to my volunteer job as a junior companion as soon as possible. I had basically the same duties, but I was also doing volunteer work at a nursing home in Yaphank, New York, through the Federation. I was a companion to elderly people, and also a companion to AIDS patients. I was really enjoying going to this nursing home. I found the work I was doing was very rewarding.

I was about fifty-one years old now. I had had my driver's license for about thirty years and had never stopped driving, even though I was a very nervous woman. I had been driving a number of different cars over the years. All of the cars that I drove were second-hand, because after my blue American Hornet, my father did help me out with getting cars. He gave a number of his cars to me as gifts over the years. I had a Plymouth at this point of my life, a small, gray car. The Plymouth that I had now was given to me by my mother as a gift. It had been her car before she stopped driving, because she was elderly now.

Through the Federation, I met another man by the name of Jeff. We started to date, but he was very sexually demanding. I knew him for only a short period of time, and he always talked about having sex with me. That kind of turned me off to him. I also had an awful lot of anxiety during this time. But, I finally gave into him. I really did not enjoy sex that much with him. I guess, maybe, I just did not trust him. I knew that in order for me to have enjoyable sex with a man, there had to be trust. Even though the sex was not enjoyable with him, it made me feel like more of a woman to have sex with a man at this point. I had had sex with other boyfriends in the past, even though I was always afraid of sex. I probably was always afraid of sex because I had been raped at a very young age.

I finally broke up with this man; we had an argument. I was attending a mental health agency in Medford at this point and was not that happy with going there. The therapist that I had there said that the relationship that I had had with this man was so short that it was considered an affair. I agreed with her. She also always told me that I needed a case manager, and I disagreed with her, because I was always a very independent person. I refused to get a case manager to help me handle all my affairs. I believed that I was perfectly capable of handling my own affairs!

There was another incident in 2003. I got on the phone and threatened suicide; I was feeling depressed and told staff members at the Federation that I felt like taking my life. A staff member called the Suffolk County Police. Again, the Fifth Precinct officers from the Suffolk County Police came to my apartment and told me that I must go to CPEP again. I was extremely upset over that. I truly believed that I was going to be kept in the hospital this time. The same officer who took me to CPEP in 2002 came to my home that day with a lady sergeant. He walked me out to the police car and handcuffed me with my hands in front. I was very upset over being handcuffed, because I was not violent and felt like I was being treated like a criminal.

On the way to the hospital, he was really nice to me. I had become very attracted to this police officer. Even though I was handcuffed, I enjoyed being with him and having a conversation with him.

Once we arrived at Stony Brook University Hospital CPEP, the handcuffs were taken off me. Again, I could have no water and I had to take off my shoes and hand over my pocketbook. I was miserable there; again, it was such a scary place, but little did I know that this visit to CPEP was a blessing in disguise! This police officer who had brought me there waited for me while I was in the waiting room for about two hours again, and he was especially nice to me. How I wished that he would like me back! Finally, I was taken in to see the doctor, and the officer said goodbye to me and left.

The doctor asked me questions about my childhood and other personal questions about my past, and I answered. I also tried to explain to the doctor that I did not mean to cry suicide; I was just upset and would never harm myself! After being evaluated for about one hour, the doctor said that I could go home! That was the grace of my God, because I truly believed that this time they were going to keep me. I went home by taxi again.

I wrote letters to this police officer who worked for the Suffolk County Police Department – Fifth Precinct, and I chased after him for about one year. I made a fool of myself; this police officer did not respond in any way. I was desperate for his love. Again, I was chasing someone who was unavailable, as during my past, I had chased after other men who were unavailable, and I became very hurt over it.

Within my sobriety, I had done a lot of work on myself, but obviously, I was still not acting the way that I wanted to. I was not the woman I wanted to be. I did want to find a good therapist and psychiatrist whom I could really trust. I wanted to find mental health professionals whom I could really work with and move ahead and get better, changing behaviors that I needed to get better from. I was sober about eighteen years now, and I felt ashamed of myself. I did not realize it at the time, but I was a sex and love addict. Later on in my life, I did seek help for this addiction.

To my surprise, another junior companion from the mental health agency where I did volunteer work highly recommended a good psychologist in Patchogue, and a good psychiatrist in Port Jefferson. I made appointments to see both of these mental health professionals and thought that maybe this was an answer to my prayers and also, maybe some good had come out of my last experience with CPEP! I was trying to look on the bright side now, and thought maybe there was still hope for me to recover. It had been a rocky road up until now with my mental illness.

When I first met my new psychologist, Doctor Kingan, I loved him and I knew that things were going to work out with him. He had a very gentle way about him and I found it very easy to talk to him about my experiences with CPEP and why I ended up there twice within the past year. And when I met my new psychiatrist, Doctor Long, I loved him, too. The psychiatric evaluation was short and he did not ask me too much about the past. He was different from most other psychiatrists I had ever met in my life! I did not feel any stigma with him. I would say that this psychiatrist was in his late sixties and he, too, had a very gentle way about him. I felt very comfortable speaking with him too about my experiences with CPEP and why I ended up there twice, and I told him that I certainly did not want to go back there. Doctor Long worked at an agency called Mather Outpatient Clinic, Port Jefferson, New York.

So as time went on, I continued seeing my new psychologist and psychiatrist. They turned out to be the best mental health professionals I had ever had, and I could see definite signs of improvement with my mental illness. I decided, too, that I was not going to cry suicide anymore and would handle my stress differently. Liking my psychiatrist so much was helping me to show big signs of improvement. Working with him was such a job. He changed my medication—he put me on Abilify, a mood stabilizer, Effexor, an antidepressant, and kept me on an anti-anxiety drug that I had been on for years, which is Klonopin. This drug is also known as an anti-psychotic drug. I was very happy with the medications and felt that Doctor Long stabilized me with the bi-polar disorder. He also helped me stop the suicide-crying. He was extremely supportive. He would counsel me for twenty minutes in his office for each visit.

I had left my volunteer job at the Federation and continued working at the nursing facility in Yaphank. I was still a companion to AIDS patients and loved it. I did this work for years. Also, it got to the point where I stopped chasing after that police officer at the Fifth Precinct. Even though I had left my volunteer job, I was still visiting with my little sweet Carmella, who was living in an adult home in Patchogue, New York. She was later on transferred to a nursing home in Patchogue, and she was now in a wheelchair. It really hurt me to see her in a wheelchair, because I loved her so dearly. I loved Carmella more than I ever loved my own biological mother, and it had gotten to the point where I referred to her as my "adopted mother."

Carmella had an Italian accent, and sometimes it was a little hard for me to understand what she was saying, but Carmella shared personal things about herself with me. She told me that she had never been married, she had no children, and had sisters who never came to see her. Her sisters were living in Brooklyn and physically not able to come to see her. Carmella and I would just tell each other how much we loved each other and laugh together. I always teased her about her big nose. Carmella never gave me advice on anything.

In 2004, I moved to another apartment in Patchogue at a really cute, really little apartment complex. At this point in my life, I had a cat by the name of Dicette. The superintendent was very nice to me; he asked me to pay one month's security instead of two months, and he did not do a background credit check. My credit was not good. To me, this apartment was beautiful, as it had a combination kitchen-living room, a little bedroom, and a cute little bathroom. The place was huge and it turned out to be the best home I had ever had, so far.

My best friend Sara suggested that I start attending Sex and Love Addicts Anonymous at this point in my life, because I had a history of chasing after unavailable men, which caused me so much pain and caused me to want to die at times.

I said to Sarah, "Why should I go to Sex and Love Addicts Anonymous? I am not a sex and love addict!"

And guess what? I started attending this program, and I kept attending it religiously. I was very dedicated to all my twelve-step programs. I still attended AA and Al-Anon programs, too, and working the three programs was doing me a world of good. As time went on, I could see that Sex and Love Addicts Anonymous was helping to relieve my unhealthy behaviors towards men. I worked with a sponsor. I got right into the steps and was showing definite signs of recovery. I worked very hard with the steps, and eventually, chasing after unavailable men did stop. I felt that, for the first time in my life, I was getting some real self-esteem and learning to love myself. Also, eventually, through my hard work with the Al-Anon Program and with Sex and Love Addicts Anonymous, that constant feeling of wanting a man in my life went away! I felt that I did not need a man in my life in order to be happy anymore. I was also working with my psychologist, Doctor Kingan, concerning my sex and love addiction.

In 2005, I started working for a political survey company; I worked on the phone talking to people all around the country every evening. This was a stressful job, but my boss and his wife told me that I was doing an excellent job! They both knew about my mental illness, but there was no stigma. And this boss was especially good to me. Within my whole life, I had never had a boss as nice as he was. Even though the job was so stressful and I did not like talking on the phone, I continued to stay at the job and grow with the job, and I made friends there. And, yes, there were co-workers who I did not get along with, but I dealt with it the best way I could. I was not getting fired!

In 2006, I returned to Suffolk County Community College in Selden. I took some political science courses there and did extremely well. I had hopes of transferring to Stony Brook State University someday, as I always wanted to go there. Stony Brook was a very hard school to get into and I had my doubts about being accepted, but Sarah kept talking positively to me.

In 2007, I got rid of an old car that I had at the time and got myself a Ford Focus, which was practically brand new. It was a 2007, previously used as a commercial car. I got it through an auto mall in Riverhead and was told that I would be paying off the car for years. My payments per month were over $500.00! The reason my payments were so high was because I had bad credit. But, this car turned out to be the best car that I had ever had in my whole life. I just loved it. It was a silver car. I gave my other car to another tenant at the apartment complex. At that time, we were friends, but that changed later on.

I started going to Goodyear Tire Center in Patchogue, New York to have my oil changes done on my new car, and other work. The staff was very nice to me over there, and every time that I had my car inspected, they could not find anything wrong with it. The staff was very honest at Goodyear.

So, I had no man in my life but I was still very happy with myself. Compared to where I was with my mental illness, I had come a long way and knew that I would continue to recover and things were just going to get better and better in my life.

Chapter Eight

In 2008, I got a job as a telemarketer in Farmingville, New York, and talk about stress! This job turned out to be the most stressful job that I had ever had in my life. I worked with a computer and a headpiece on me—taking one phone call after another. I sold the *Daily News*. A lot of people got very nasty with me on the phone. Some people would even curse at me, and sometimes, I had obscene things said to me. But, the good thing about this job was that the two bosses I worked for were really nice to me. These bosses were always smiling and it turned out to be a real fun place to work. Co-workers were always joking around. Even though I did not get along with everyone, most of my co-workers I got along with. And the boss that I worked with in the evenings became very close as a friend, and I could see that he had a personal interest in me. He was about thirty-nine years old and he was just such a nice man to work for. Sometimes, I would work during the day with the other boss. And that was fun, too. I was about fifty-six years old now. This job played a very big role within my mental health recovery.

That same year, I was accepted into Stony Brook State University in Stony Brook, New York. This was just about the best thing that had ever happened to me in my sobriety and recovery from mental illness! I transferred from Suffolk County Community College in Selden, New York. This was one of the happiest times of my life! My people within the Twelve Step programs were so happy for me and told me that they knew that I would be accepted, and of course, my best friend Sarah was so happy for me. I found out at orientation that out of 25,000 students who had applied to Stony Brook University at the time, only 2,700 students were selected—and I was one of them.

I truly believe that it was through the grace of God that I got into that school, as I had some D+s on my transcript from Suffolk County Community College. I was a walking miracle.

Although I started Stony Brook University in September, I still worked as a telemarketer for the *Daily News*. I was really surprised that I had never gotten fired from that job. I never believed that my sales were that great, but then again, the bosses were willing to work with me, and they were also very sensitive to my mental illness.

My first semester at Stony Brook was extremely stressful for me. I decided to take a one-credit course, which was Introduction to Stony Brook (SBU 101), and I also took a Colonial Latin America course (History 213). I found this course to be very interesting; it was about the history of Latin American from the fifteenth century on, and the professor and teacher's assistant seemed nice. I got 100% on my first quiz and I was so happy! A long time ago, while growing up, I was told that I was not capable of going to college. Now I was attending one of the best schools and one of the hardest schools in the country. Obviously, there was a big misunderstanding with my parents.

I ended up doing a large presentation in this class in front of over 200 students and yes, I was very nervous and I stammered, but got through it; the professor congratulated me and was so proud of me for volunteering to do this presentation, despite my problem with stammering. The next semester, Spring 2009, I took The Legend of King Arthur (MVL 141). This course was about knights. I felt that I was not doing well in this course and ended up getting 26% on the first test. I was absolutely devastated. I was registered with Disability Support Services and went over there to speak to my counselor and was crying my eyes out. She helped me by giving me a lot of support; I also had a counselor in Student Advisory Center, and both of these counselors told me not to give up and to keep on coming back to the University. Somehow, through the grace of God, I managed to pull my test grades up in this course and ended up getting a C+. I was pretty much satisfied with the grade, and I continued on with Stony Brook University.

Down the road, I ended up taking two Biology courses, one per semester, which I really enjoyed. I had the same wonderful professor for both of the Biology courses, the Living World (BIO 150) and Human Biology (BIO 101). I became very close to this professor as a friend and e-mailed him all of the time and he would e-mail me back. I always took my summers off and did not attend school, as I felt that I was not ready to attend school all year round.

There came a semester in 2010 when I started taking two courses at a time. I took a Feminist course called Women, Culture and Difference (WST 103) and World Politics (POL 101). A lot of the Feminist course content had to do with women's struggles within this country to gain their rights. The Political Science course was all about World War I and World War II. I really enjoyed the reading, but the course was just straight multiple choice question tests and I did not do well. I just did not care for the professor, either. I really struggled with this course and worked very hard to pull my grade up. I ended up getting a D in this course. I did enjoy the Feminist course, and gave a presentation in that course in front of a lot of students; I got a B- in the course. I was always getting support from my counselors in Disability Support Services and the Academic Advisory Counseling Center. I continued on at Stony Brook, even though it was a struggle and my anxiety level was always very high during the semesters. And I managed to continue to work as a telemarketer and attend the University at the same time.

Chapter Nine

It came to the point within my recovery from mental illness when I wanted to work with the mentally ill; I felt ready for it, and I felt that I had enough recovery. I spoke to my psychologist and psychiatrist about this. Both of them agreed that I was able to work with the mentally ill. I had gone on some interviews for a Peer Specialist position and finally, in April of 2010, I was hired as a Peer Specialist at a human services agency in Bay Shore, New York.

I started this position on the twenty-seventh of that month and the position was part-time. I worked on Tuesdays, Thursdays, and Fridays. I was so very happy about getting this position; I felt that this was one of the best things that had ever happened to me so far in my sobriety and mental health recovery.

During the course of the workdays, I visited different adult homes in the Town of Islip, to lead groups with residents, and to talk to residents on a one-to-one basis. I shared a little office with three case managers at the human services agency in Bay Shore. I did feel a little uncomfortable sitting so closely with three other people who were strangers to me, but I used my Twelve Steps programs of recovery, especially Al-Anon.

Things seemed to go very well at first, and the Program Director and Program Coordinator who hired me seemed to be very happy with me. I was not feeling any stress at this job for about the first six months and referred to it as the job of my dreams.

After I was on this job for about a month, my sweet Carmella passed away in an Extended Care Facility in Uniondale, New York. I got a phone call one day from one of the staff members there. Carmella had no one but me, and that is why I was called.

I was devastated and I cried a lot. I arranged her funeral with a funeral director named Anthony LiCausi from Robertaccio Funeral Home in Patchogue. This particular funeral home buried people who had no money. Carmella had no wake, but she was given a gray casket, and she wore a pretty black dress that the funeral home director bought for her. I was so grateful to that funeral home. My Carmella had a beautiful service at Holy Sepulchre Cemetery in Coram, NY. After my Carmella was buried, I continued to cry and felt that I had a knot in my stomach for the longest time. I attended a bereavement group for a while and it helped.

After I was on my job for a couple of months, I was told that I could drive the company van. I was so afraid of driving the van, because I had never driven a van in my life. The lady who was my AA sponsor at the time gave me a lot of encouragement and support. She kept telling me that if I could drive a car, then I could drive the van. She kept telling me that I could do it. Finally, one day, one of the male case managers from the office took me out in the van. I then drove it with him in it and found that it was not all that bad.

From then on, I started driving the van, and also started taking agency clients from the adult homes on outings. Some of the places I took clients to were the movies, Burger King, McDonald's, and later on, parks. I really enjoyed these outings with the clients, even though I had a lot of anxiety while doing it.

I started having a lot of difficulty with one of the case managers who worked in the office with me. And this was really hard for me, because we worked so closely. She was a very moody person and under so much stress. She started walking in every morning and not saying hello to me—just a faint, "Hello." She also started getting abrupt with me a lot. She was an abrupt person, but I guess I was taking it personally, for I am a very sensitive soul. The situation would get worse with her, and then better. One day, we had words over a client. I was extremely upset over this and felt like walking out. This situation was upsetting my serenity. I tried talking to the Program Coordinator about this case manager a number of times, but she did nothing to help me. This Program Coordinator was my immediate supervisor and she was turning out to be an abrupt person herself at times, because of her workload.

I felt that I was mixing pain with pleasure because I really loved my job. I loved the paperwork and I loved working with the clients, but some of the personalities within the office I had such difficulties with. Of course, I got support from women in both programs; AA and Al-Anon were both helping me to recover. I also did a lot of praying to my God. I felt that God was with me through it all.

Things just continued to get worse in the office with the personality conflicts but also, as time went on, I felt a lot of stress as far as the paperwork and outings with clients. It seemed that the longer I was on the job, the more was expected of me, and it finally got to the point at times where the pressure seemed intolerable. I was making good money at this job—$16.48 per hour—and did not want to resign. I was told by other staff people in the department that everyone was feeling the pressure. Obviously, it was a very demanding agency.

One day, the case manager whom I was having difficulties with shared with me that she was looking for another job. She told me that she could not handle the stress on the job any longer, as it was too much for her. I also told her that maybe I should look for another job, too. And we got into a big conversation. There were days that I had to take off from work because of the stress, and my psychologist was very supportive. My psychiatrist kept telling me that I could do the job and I resented that.

In January 2011, I started attending a rehabilitation center in Patchogue, New York, for physical therapy. I had pain in my lower back and legs. The physical therapy helped me a lot. I was taught exercises to do at home. Every time I attended physical therapy, I did exercises on different machines, and different physical therapists massaged my back and stretched my legs from one direction to another.

In addition to my job and physical therapy, I still attended Stony Brook University, and I was doing very well by now. I changed my curriculum from Political Science to History. I was now a History Major. Apparently, I had taken a History course along the way called United States Since 1877 (HIS 104) and had fallen in love with American History all over again! This course was a lot about what happened before World War I, including immigration, World War I, and what happened within this country after World War I.

I had always done well in History courses in high school. I was under a lot of stress during the semesters, but no matter how much stress I was under, I just kept trying and continuing my education at Stony Brook University. I was also in and out of Disability Support Services. Every time I would go there to see my counselor, I would have to fill out a little slip with the question: Reason for Visit? And I would write down: Support! I always needed my counselor to tell me that I was going to graduate someday, as I lacked the confidence and I was still afraid of failing. But, my grades were very good at this point. And in History 104, I ended up getting an A!

In April 2011, my darling cat Dicette died of cancer. I had to have her put to sleep at the animal hospital in Holbrook. I had been going to this animal hospital for the past seventeen years with all of the adult cats that I had. When Dicette died, I felt that I did not want to go on any longer without her, but I just bore the pain. I went to work daily in a lot of pain. I was functioning with the tools of Doctor Low's Recovery Program. I did not want to adopt another adult cat right away. One Sunday morning, the following month, I got a phone call from a friend in AA asking me to come to her home to see kittens rescued from a home where they were being abused. Her daughter had rescued them. I told my friend that I was not ready to adopt another cat. And I certainly did not want a kitten, as I felt that I did not have the patience to take care of a kitten.

I decided to go to my friend's home anyway, in Patchogue, to see the kittens; there were three beautiful kittens in a box. Two of them were gray and one of them was black. I fell in love with these kittens. My friend's daughter told me that where these kittens were living, the owners were giving them beer to drink, dog food to eat, and children were hitting them.

That evening, two kittens were sitting on my living room couch—I had brought a gray one and the black one home! The gray one was a girl and the black one was a boy cat. I named them Sophie and Barney. I ended up having a lot of patience with them, even though they were so noisy and tore at things in my apartment!

During the summer of 2011, I did not attend Stony Brook University and I really enjoyed my summer off. I planned to take two History Courses the following September 2011. And I was always afraid of starting school again. That fear of failure was with me all the time.

In July of the same year, I celebrated twenty-six years of sobriety at my AA group in Holbrook. It was a blast, and I was so very happy. It seemed that this was the best AA sober anniversary that I had ever had, and I really loved my group. Twenty-six years of sobriety was a long, long time and I was so very proud of myself and thankful to my God for helping me to stay sober for that amount of time.

At my job, the situation was not getting any better in the department. And staff members kept telling me that I was not the only one feeling the stress—everyone was feeling the stress. It just got to the point where my immediate supervisor was so busy all the time that I could not even ask her questions, and I started to resent her. And every time I had to take clients on outings, I had to type out service dollar requests and have them signed by the case managers in the office I worked in, and then by my supervisor. I then had to get money from the staff person who handled the service dollar requests and gave out the money. She always got abrupt with me, too. I am sure that it was nothing personal, but it still was affecting me very badly.

I kept taking days off from my job at times because it felt like my head was going to explode—that is how much pressure I was under. I was truly thinking of resigning, as I was a nervous wreck all of the time and my anxiety level was sky-high all of the time.

In September, 2011, I went back to Stony Brook University and took two American History Courses: American History to 1877 (HIS 103), which was about what happened before the Revolutionary War; and the Revolutionary War and Reading and Writing History (HIS 301), which was about the making of the Atomic Bomb. I found it very hard to keep up with that job and school. My professor in 103 noticed that there was something wrong—as I got nasty with her one day. I then apologized to her and told her about the situation at my job. She really understood. I really loved this professor; she was extremely kind to me and to the other students in the class.

That October, I celebrated my sixtieth birthday! What a big event, and I was so happy to be alive! I could not believe that I had survived everything that I had experienced in my life, especially my horrible childhood and the rape when I was six years old. I was rejoicing.

Chapter Ten

One day in November 2011, I came into work and when I checked my mail on the computer, I found that there was a message about the case manager whom I did not like. The message said that she was resigning from the agency that December. Oh, my God, I could not believe it. I felt that my prayers were answered. I was so relieved, but knew that I had to put up with her moods a while longer. I later found out that the other female case manager in our little office also was going to resign at the end of December. She was resigning because of the same reason that the other case manager was resigning—stress and feeling overworked.

I continued to talk to my psychologist about my job. I had been seeing him for about nine years now. I really loved him. He shared with me that he had similar experiences at his jobs that I was having now at my job, and he had never had any luck working with other people and with bosses. He told me that that was why he had his own office now!

I did make a decision, with the help of my dear psychologist, to resign from my job and to continue moving on with my beautiful life. It was not the end of the world. And resigning from this job really did not have anything to do with my mental illness, as two other people resigned at the same time from the same agency for the same reasons. I feared another mental breakdown, also; despite the fact that I was that I was making $650.00 bi-weekly, it was not worth my mental health, and the job was changing my whole personality.

I did resign on December 12, 2011. After I left the agency, I felt that a weight was taken off my shoulders. I did not miss it there at all and felt no loss. I did continue visiting, on a volunteer basis, with the residents who lived in the adult homes, and I was really loved by them. They said that they really enjoyed my visits.

I decided that I probably would not go back to work until I received my Bachelor's Degree in History from Stony Brook State University. I had definite plans of becoming a rehabilitation counselor one day, and continuing my work with the mentally ill. People in my Twelve Step programs—AA and Al-Anon—kept telling me that I could do it, and my psychologist and psychiatrist were very supportive, too. Just because the job at the human services agency in Bay Shore was not suitable for me, it did not mean that I could not find another job someday where I would be happier.

At this point in my life, I was living off my disability benefits from Social Security. I would also receive a huge disbursement check from Stony Brook University from the loans that I kept taking out. The disbursement check would be thousands of dollars and that would hold me over for quite some time.

In January 2012, I became a published author and Charles Day, from the same human services agency that I worked at, helped me to achieve that goal! Charles Day was an ombudsman of Suffolk County for adult homes and he worked in the main office of the agency in Huntington, New York. He edited the story of my life, which is called *I Lived in Hope*. This beautiful story went into an anthology called *Mental Wellness: Real Stories from Survivors* and the book ended up getting published. About eleven other mental illness survivors wrote stories for this book, and Charles kept telling me that the book was selling well. And I also sold copies of the book to a lot of business associates in Patchogue, such as the florist, deli, funeral home that buried Carmella, auto service center, etc. Many more business associates of mine bought the book.

Now that I was not working, Stony Brook University, aside from AA and Al-Anon, was a major priority in my life. I was really having a great time with waking up in the mornings and attending school. My life had become a blast now! And after I left my job at the human services agency, I calmed down so much and my anxiety level was so much better. Even my professor in HIS 103 noticed a drastic change in me.

The end of the fall semester finally came. I took my final exams for HIS 103 and HIS 301; Reading and Writing History had no tests or final at all. I just had to do a ten-page term paper. I did my paper on Albert Einstein. I had always loved him because I identified with him; he did not have a good childhood, either. He had a very rough time in school and the other children made fun of him, but he turned out to be brilliant. I did not earn the Writing Requirement for graduation from this term paper, but I took it with grace. I did not lose my temper or get that upset. I ended up earning a B+ in HIS 103 and a B in HIS 301. And I knew that I would get the Writing Requirement some other time before graduation. I had heard that a lot of students did not get the Writing Requirement the first try.

The Writing Requirement for students who attend Stony Brook State University entails writing a research paper of at least ten pages about a certain important subject whom we had researched. We were expected to get at least a B on the paper in order to receive what is called the Writing Requirement, which we have to get in order to graduate with a Bachelor's Degree.

I was very happy with the progress I had made with my mental health recovery. This was the best that I had ever been in my whole life so far, and I had such peace and serenity. My little Barney and Sophie were about nine months old now, and next to AA and Al-Anon, they were the love of my life! Although they were both tearing up my furniture and my bed in the bedroom, I just loved them so much and accepted them just the way they were, including with their claws. I kept in close contact with the animal hospital in Holbrook. I was friends with the staff there. Barney and Sophie turned out to be the best experience that I had ever had with cats that I had adopted!

I had come so far with my angry temper, even though I had had anger issues all of my life. I was handling situations much better now, including tailgaters on the road. I was not responding with anger any more, like I used to. I was coping so much better now with everything that came my way. The only thing that ever helped with my anger was getting down on my knees every morning and asking God to arrest it, one day at a time, and working with the Sixth Step of recovery, "Were entirely ready to ask God to remove all of our character defects," because the way I use to handle my anger was a character defect. And all of my shortcomings had gotten so much better, too.

In January 2012, the Spring Semester started at Stony Brook University and of course, my anxiety level was high again. It was always hard for me to start a new semester.

I was now taking Early Republic (HIS 264) and Civil War and Reconstruction (HIS 265). HIS 264 was about what happened within this country before the Revolutionary War, during the Revolutionary War, and afterward. HIS 265 was about slavery, the Civil War, and what occurred within this country after the Civil War, or Reconstruction.

I enjoyed both of these courses, but still had the fear of failing. I still spoke to my Disability Support Services Counselor frequently. She assured me that I was going to definitely graduate someday. I was hanging in there and just showing up for all of my classes. In HIS 265, the slavery issue was very sad to me. I felt so sorry for what the poor slaves went through in this country. I was feeling a lot of emotions over this.

Professor Donna Rilling taught the HIS 264 course, and Professor Bill Miller taught the HIS 265 course. Little did I know that these two professors would become very instrumental in my success at Stony Brook University. Professor Bill Miller seemed like a nice man, but Professor Donna Rilling seemed to be a hard professor to me, at first, and I was a little bit afraid of her.

Meanwhile, I had seen my doctor, Ashley Lewin, Naturopathic Physician, at the end of January, 2012 and had a long talk with her about the foods that I was eating. I had had an eating disorder all of my life and kept falling back into the same bad eating habits, but this time, I hoped that I could stick to a good meal plan. I was also a sugar addict all of my life and it was at the point where any sugar-related substances made me feel ill. Sugar made me shake and gave me a lot more anxiety. That day in Doctor Lewin's office, she set up a whole new meal plan for me, which consisted of frying all of my foods with olive oil, butter, onions, and garlic in a frying pan; some of the fried foods were eggs, bacon, meat, and vegetables. Foods that I was eating and did not fry were cottage cheese, whole plain low- or no-fat yogurt, cucumbers, and very limited fruits.

After I saw Doctor Lewin in her office that day, it was as if I started a whole new life with my food, and I was sixty years old. Doctor Lewin told me that good nutrition was very important for good mental health and for the control of anxiety. I told her that I never knew that. I followed this meal plan to a T and felt better quickly. And, I was staying away from the sugar, one day at a time. Also, every morning when I got down on my knees, I asked God to help me keep the sugar under control, one day at a time, and the food. So far, this was working for me. This was the best meal plan that I had ever been on in all my life and it came in *God's* time, not in my time. Doctor Lewin also told me that I could take amino acids for my anxiety, which supplement was available in the health food store in Sayville, New York.

As time went on with school, I could see that Professor Bill Miller was giving me a lot of emotional support. I kept e-mailing him all of the time and telling him that I was afraid to raise my hand in class, although I wanted to. He kept encouraging me to do so. I was really getting to know him and I could see that he was helping an awful lot of students in his office hours, too.

I was starting to like Professor Donna Rilling, because I could see that she was really sensitive to my mental illness. One day when I was in her office for office hours, she handed an essay back to me that I had typed up and told me that it was a failing essay. She asked me if I would re-do the essay and go to the Writing Center, which was on Stony Brook University Campus, for help. I told her that I would re-do the essay with the help of a tutor at the Writing Center.

I worked very hard on the essay with the help of a tutor from the Writing Center and kept telling Professor Donna Rilling how the essay was coming along. I could see that she was pleased with my efforts. I finally handed the essay into her again and ended up getting a B on it. I was so very happy about that.

I had my midterm in HIS 264 in March 2012 and was very nervous about how I did. When I took the midterm in Disability Support Services, I was very ill that day with a stomach virus and had a lot of anxiety and was forgetting information that I had studied. I waited with a lot of anxiety to get my exam back and found out that I got a 90% on the test, or an A-! I was so very happy and knew that God was doing for me what I could not do for myself. And in HIS 265, I had my first take-home exam, which was an essay; I was very nervous about this. I ended up getting an A- on that essay. Wow! I was really doing well at Stony Brook University at this point.

As time went on, I was got to know Professor Bill Miller and Professor Donna Rilling a lot better and I just loved the both of them, as they had been very supportive of me. I truly believed that they were both wonderful people, aside from being good professors. At the end of the semester, I received a B in HIS 264 and an A in HIS 265. I was very pleased with that.

My cats, Barney and Sophie, were about a year old now and we seemed to have a very happy family. They too, like myself, came from an alcoholic home and somehow, we found each other. These two cats were so very happy with me and ran through my apartment rooms screaming daily. I loved them to death. All cats are beautiful, but my Barney and Sophie were the most beautiful cats that I have ever seen! My God is a God of Miracles and works in very mysterious ways. I felt at that time that if Dicette had not died, I would not have had these two beautiful kittens now.

Chapter Eleven

I decided to attend Stony Brook University in the summer session of 2012. It started at the end of May of that year. I had to take a language in order to graduate with a Bachelor's Degree in History, so I decided to take sign language, and the Elementary American Sign Language courses, SLN 111 and SLN 112, were offered only during the summer sessions at Stony Brook University.

My first day of this course, I was having a rough time learning the teacher's signs. The other students in the class were much younger than I was. They really seemed to understand the teacher well. After the class, I spoke to the teacher and told her that I was having difficulty and she told me that it was my age. She told me that older students taking the elementary sign language course usually had difficulty understanding the signs. She suggested that I drop out, but I told her that I was going to continue with the Elementary American Sign Language I course, and that is just what I did. I showed up every Tuesday and Thursday mornings for class and was learning, but very slowly.

In this class, we had to mingle with other students and practice the sign language and this was hard for me. At times, we had to stand up in front of the room with partners and carry on conversations in sign language. My anxiety and nervousness were so high, but I kept on persevering.

I studied the sign language very hard at home, watched the sign language tapes at Stony Brook University Melville Library, and I even got a tutor. The tutor who I had come to my home was in AA. I paid her to tutor me. With everything that I did to pass this sign language course, I was still failing every test. My nervousness was getting in the way. The Elementary Sign Language I course was only four weeks long, because it was given during the summertime. I did not go on to the second part of this course because I received a D for the first part of the course. I was very glad that I received a D and not an F. I planned to take sign language again at Stony Brook University the following summer of 2013. I was proud of myself for trying.

Aside from attending classes in the summertime for sign language, I thought about moving from my apartment in Patchogue. Outside the apartment building, there were very unsanitary conditions, and the neighbors were not that friendly. Sarah kept telling me, "Go to The Waterfalls! Go to The Waterfalls! So-and-so in AA has been living there for five years now and loves it there."

The Waterfalls was a community in Lake Ronkonkoma; I had never seen it, but it sounded like a nice place to live.

I finally got on the phone and called The Waterfalls Community one day, and a lady on the other end of the phone told me to come down to see the community, and she gave me directions.

When I went to The Waterfalls at the beginning of July, 2012, I was breathless because this community was so very beautiful and it was huge! There were two different waterfalls. The trees and the flowers all over the community were just so lovely, and I really wanted to live there. The office was in a huge building on top of a hill and the building looked like a mansion.

The property manager, named Jane, showed me an apartment and said to me, "Do you like it?"

I said, "Yes."

"Then it is yours, Elizabeth."

I was so very happy. This apartment was beautiful and perfect for one person. It was a one-bedroom apartment, and it had a full kitchen, living room, and a nice-sized bathroom.

We went back to Jane's office to talk, and she told me that it was going to be two months' security. She said that she would work out a payment plan with me. I told her that I had two cats, and she was disturbed by that, but said that she would give me an apartment facing the woods so that no one would see the cats. She said that it was an animal-free community, but that a lot of tenants had cats.

I drove over to the Section 8 office in Patchogue and informed my caseworker that I had found an apartment, and where. My caseworker was happy for me, but said that my case had to be transferred to the Town of Brookhaven, the Section 8 office in Farmingville, New York. I was going to be living in Lake Ronkonkoma now.

After the apartment at The Waterfalls was inspected by an inspector from the Town of Brookhaven, Jane let me move in on July 15. Doctor Lewin, her significant other, and her daughter moved me to my new home. I thought that Barney and Sophie would be very happy there, but that did not turn out to be the case.

Barney and Sophie started having adjustment problems as soon as I moved in. Barney's behavior was much worse than Sophie's. Barney cried constantly day and night, and jumped up on the apartment wall by the door and scratched it. He was also doing a lot of hiding, and Sophie was hiding, too. I called the animal hospital in Holbrook for support; they told me that the cats would eventually get used to the place, but that it was going to take time. As time went on, Barney's crying got worse, to the point where I was up at nights with him, petting him and hoping that he would calm down.

Finally, I took him to a veterinarian in Speonk, New York. He was highly recommended to me by one of Doctor Lewin's secretaries. This doctor in Speonk dealt with homeopathic medicine for animals. I believed that Barney needed medication to calm down.

When I took Barney to see this doctor in Speonk, the doctor examined Barney while I told him what the problem was. He said that Barney was having a lot of anxiety; I told him that Barney was never like this until I moved. The doctor said that I was to give him two tablets for anxiety twice a day.

I did what this doctor said, but it was very hard for me to give Barney the medication, as he was very upset by this. As time went on, it seemed as if the medication was working, but then, Barney seemed to be getting worse again with the crying. He also scratched the walls by my apartment's inside and outside doors, and seemed to be having fits. This really affected me. One day, when I saw my psychologist in his office,

Doctor Kingan told me that Barney would get better in time and probably did not need to have pills shoved down his throat.

Meanwhile, the Fall semester of 2012 got started at Stony Brook University. I took American Slavery in the Atlantic World (HIS 396) and Environmental History in Global Perspective (HIS 302). Professor Jennifer Anderson taught the course HIS 396, and Professor Alix Cooper taught HIS 302. They both seemed like very friendly people.

HIS 396 was about how slavery first got started as slaves were taken to the Americas by ships, and also about slavery in the thirteen northern and southern colonies. I found this course to be very interesting, as were many other courses that I had taken at Stony Brook. Also, I felt that I was getting a very intensive education about slavery.

HIS 302 was a lot about the development of environments in different parts of the world. The information in the beginning of this course went back to ancient times. The course was also about certain types of animals. I really enjoyed this course, too. I also had another opportunity to get the Writing Requirement now, by typing up a ten-page research paper in for this course.

I discussed what kind of research paper I wanted to do with Professor Cooper; I told her that I wanted to do my research paper on something that had to do with slavery. She suggested that I do my paper on Environment and Slavery, and I agreed to that. I wanted the Writing Requirement so badly, as it was very important for graduation.

Meanwhile, it was very hard for me to study and to do my schoolwork at home because of Barney's crying. I noticed that both Barney and Sophie kept going to my apartment's inside door. I guess that they both wanted to go out. Barney and Sophie were also always at the door of my other apartment, but never went out. The owner of that community did not allow tenants to let our cats outside. Doctor Lewin suggested that I start taking Barney outdoors because of his anxiety, so I went to the pet shop in town and bought him a harness and a leash. I trained him inside the apartment to walk with the leash, then I started taking him to a park in Lake Ronkonkoma. He seemed to enjoy the outdoors, and his anxiety seemed to get better again, at first. Sophie was much too heavy; it was too difficult for me to take her out every single day. It would hurt my back, but Sophie was not doing any crying. She was mostly just hiding in the bathtub and the closets.

I started working on my research paper for HIS 302, and I was getting a lot of help and support from Professor Alix Cooper. She was with me every step of the way. She just kept making corrections on my paper and I followed the corrections and kept typing the paper over and over again. I was so determined.

I also still got a lot of emotional support at Disability Support Services from the counselors, Wendi and Kathy. I still took all of my exams in there. I really loved the staff in Disability Support Services.

Professor Bill Miller, who is the Director of the Undergraduate Program at Stony Brook for the History Department, offered to read my ten-page research paper. He wanted me to get the Writing Requirement this time. He was being very supportive. I gave the paper to him to read. He found a lot of mistakes on my paper and made comments on it, but I continued working with Professor Alix Cooper.

Working on this research paper caused me an awful lot of stress and anxiety, but I kept on persevering. I was not going to give up and was determined to get the Writing Requirement so that I could graduate from Stony Brook with my Bachelor's Degree. I not only got support from Professor Bill Miller and Professor Alix Cooper, I also got a lot of support from people in AA and Al-Anon, and of course, from my favorite friend, Sarah, and she was about eighty years old now! Sarah was a sister to me.

After my research paper was done, I handed it to Professor Alix Cooper and she signed a yellow paper for the History Department, and she said that she would give it to Professor Bill Miller to sign, too. I was very happy about this. Later, Professor Bill Miller e-mailed me to congratulate me and told me that I fulfilled the Writing Requirement. My mark on this paper was a B, but I was satisfied, as I knew that I did the best job that I could. I also received an A in the History 396 course and a B+ in the History 302 course.

At the end of January, 2013, the Spring semester started at Stony Brook University and I took Black Pop Culture and the Terrain (AFS 320) and Germany, 1890 to 1945 (HIS 312). I wanted to take a course about the history of Germany because I am half-German, and my great-grandparents on my father's side were from Germany.

AFS 320 was about the black peoples' struggles within this country for justice and equality. On the first day of class with this course, I found out that I was going to have to do an oral presentation with two other colleagues and I was extremely nervous about that.

As far as the HIS 312 Course was concerned, it was about the history of Germany before World War I, a little bit about World War I, what happened before World War II in Germany, and World War II. This course was also about the holocaust that took place in German Southwest Africa in 1904 to 1907 in which the German Militia killed Nama and Herero peoples, and the Holocaust that took place throughout Europe from 1941 to 1945 with the killing of millions of Jews by Nazi Germany. During this course, all of us students in the class saw films about Adolf Hitler and in the films, crowds of people were screaming, "Heil Hitler! Heil Hitler!" I was getting tired of hearing, "Heil Hitler!" The information that we learned, about what took place during the Holocaust, was very sad. I just had to grin and bear it. I decided that one course about Adolf Hitler was enough!

In February 2013, there was a major snowstorm. I had never seen so much snow in all my life. But, the snow looked beautiful and the woods and hills in back of my apartment were covered with snow and it looked like a wonderland. A neighbor named Hank shoveled out my car from the snow and I was very grateful to him.

The neighbors were pretty nice at The Waterfalls and I made friends with the next-door neighbor, named Larry, and his son, Jeff. Larry had had four strokes and was confined to a scooter. I visited with him practically every day. Larry had a grandson named Anthony, about eight years old when I first met him. I fell in love with this child, as he was a little doll and he was very kind to me. Anthony loved me, too; he told me so. We always hugged.

After this snowstorm, I did not have any school for about one week and I missed school, but I continued attending my Twelve Step program meetings. For me, my meetings were a matter of life or death.

I could not take Barney out to walk and was having a lot of difficulty handling his behavior. The cat wanted to go out, but I knew that if I took him to the park with the snow on the ground, the ground would be too cold for him and he would not walk. I made every effort to keep Barney, as I loved him so much and did not want to give him up. I felt that I could not bear to live without him.

Although it was freezing outside at this time of year, I still managed to walk from one building to another to get to my classes, after I returned to school. I suffered from lower back pain and pain in my right leg. I just bore the pain. I truly believed that God and the Blessed Virgin Mary were helping me through Stony Brook State University. Going to school there for the past five and a half years was certainly a major challenge for me, mentally and even physically.

I still e-mailed Professor Donna Rilling at times for support, and she e-mailed me back. She was such a support to me. I think I really knew Professor Donna Rilling better than many other students knew her. She had a very kind heart.

I really struggled with my schoolwork during the Spring semester, as I found it very difficult to keep up. I did do an oral presentation in AFS 320 about the narrative, *Running a Thousand Miles for Freedom,* which was the story of a married couple who escaped from slavery. I did the oral presentation with two other students. I had butterflies in my stomach and boy, was I nervous, but got through it.

In HIS 312, we had quizzes in the course and I failed every quiz, but I passed every exam, as the professor was curving the exams. I really did enjoy the professor's lectures in HIS 312. I found the class to be very interesting, but I would never really know the real reason why my great-grandparents came to the United States from where they were living in Germany. At the end of the Spring semester, I visited with the Academic Advisory Counseling Department a number of times and found out that I needed about twenty-four more credits in order to graduate from the university. I would probably graduate in about two more years.

After school was over for the semester, I received a B in AFS 320 and a B- in HIS 312.

I decided not to go to school for the summer of 2013, because I had had a rough semester prior to this. I decided to take a break. I started doing some volunteer work for the National Multiple Sclerosis Society, Long Island Chapter, in Melville, New York and I really enjoyed it. I did weekly mailings and other little tasks in a beautiful office. A young lady by the name of Sarah Lutz was my volunteer coordinator. Sarah had the same first name as my best friend. Sarah, at this volunteer job, was especially kind to me and knew about my past struggles with mental illness. I also was meeting a lot of lovely people at this volunteer job.

Also, in May 2013, I was scheduled for a colonoscopy at a gastroenterologist's office in Port Jefferson Station, New York. I made the appointment for this with Doctor Allen, as it had been eleven years since my last colonoscopy and my grandmother, Samantha, had colon cancer before she had died. I did a one-day preparation, and then my AA sponsor drove me to the gastroenterologist office to have this procedure done.

That day, I was put under anesthesia; I remember waking up and being told that the colonoscopy could not be done because I was not all cleaned out. Before I left the office that day, I was told that I was going to have to come back in about three weeks, and I was going to have to do a three-day preparation and use a solution that was given to me that day. I was very upset over that. I could not imagine doing a three-day preparation.

I continued taking Barney for walks every day in a park in Lake Ronkonkoma and thought that he was enjoying the walks, as it got him out of the apartment, but it only helped a little. He still seemed to have a lot of anxiety at home and now, Sophie showed signs of anxiety, too. She cried in the evenings at times, and went into the closet by the apartment inside door and cried and bang around. It seemed as if she was copying Barney's behaviors.

I did the three-day preparation, then went back to the gastroenterologist's office. It was horrible and I felt that I was going to die. I was so weak and dizzy. I had to drink fluids and solutions for three days, and did not eat any solid foods. A friend of mine from AA took me for this test. After the colonoscopy, I was told that everything was normal in my colon and there was no sign of cancer and boy, was I relieved. A colonoscopy is a very good procedure for anyone to have done.

One day, in June, 2013, I received a letter in the mail from one of the owners of The Waterfalls Community telling me that I had to find another home for my pets, because it was a pet-free community. I was startled and did not know how he found out that I had pets unless Jane, the former manager, had it written down somewhere. There was a new property manager now, named Linda, and she was extremely nice.

I did not know where to start to find a home for my Barney and Sophie. On one hand, I loved them so much, but on the other hand, I knew that finding an owner who had a house for them was for the best. I wanted to give them a better life, and being cooped up in an apartment was no life for either one of them. I knew that I had to plan, decide, and act, fast. I contacted Doctor Lewin and she said that she knew of some people who may be able to give Barney and Sophie the kind of home that they deserved and needed.

In a matter of a couple of days, Doctor Lewin told me that she had found a home for Barney and Sophie with an acquaintance of hers. This woman had a house in Mattituck, New York and she also had a barn. Barney and Sophie would stay in the barn at first, until they were ready to go outside. I was very grateful to Doctor Lewin for helping me find my cats a more suitable home. I knew that the new living situation would probably help their anxiety. I wanted to free them.

That June day, I drove Barney and Sophie in their carriers and their toys and other belongings up to Doctor Lewin's office in Riverhead, New York. Doctor Lewin was waiting for me in her mini-van. I took both of the carriers, with Barney and Sophie in them, and Doctor Lewin put Barney and Sophie in the back of her mini-van. I also gave her their toys and other belongings and I said goodbye to the both of them and it was very sad. On one hand, I was relieved, but on the other hand, I knew that I was going to miss the both of them terribly.

I went through a heavy grieving period for about one month over Barney and Sophie. Certain mornings, I would wake up and think that I heard Barney crying. It was so quiet in my apartment now. I missed the fun that I use to have with them, as they were very loveable, but I knew that it was for the best that they had a better home now. They needed a home where they could go outside and run and play. I never saw them again and I was sad about that, but knew that they were probably having a lot of fun now in their new home in Mattituck, New York.

Epilogue

Even though I had to give up Barney and Sophie, my life is still beyond my wildest dreams today and I have never been happier in my whole life. I do have financial problems, but I still have a lot of peace and serenity today. As time goes on, I just seem to be getting better and better, and my life is getting better and better. What more can I ask for? My food addiction is much better now and I have recovered from my fears of men. Over the past twenty-eight years of my sobriety, my anger issues have gotten so much better, and I very rarely lose my temper at this point in my life. I have worked so hard to become the kind of person I want to be. But, the work is not over. It will never be over. I am continuously working the Twelve Steps of recovery.

I try the best I can to take care of myself today from head to foot. I still receive mental health treatment, and I found an excellent primary care physician in Nesconset with whom I am very pleased. His name is Doctor Little, and he seems to be very sensitive to my feelings, and he actually speaks with his patients on the phone. A lot of doctors do not. He is treating me for a minor thyroid condition and I take a medication called Levothyroxine for this condition.

I started seeing a podiatrist located in Patchogue, New York, because I have calluses on my feet. I am taking care of my feet and this podiatrist has helped me. This doctor is a very nice man and I like him a lot.

I also have gone back for physical therapy, but at a rehabilitation center in Smithtown, New York. I went back for this treatment because, again, I was having pain in my lower back and legs. This physical therapy is very intense, more intense than I was having at the rehabilitation center in Patchogue, New York. It is strenuous, but it is helping me. I exercise on different machines and the physical therapist, Frank, stretches my legs in different directions.

I take care of myself by having a life insurance policy today. I have pre-funeral arrangements at Robertaccio Funeral Home in Patchogue, New York. Anthony LiCausi is my funeral director and he is also my friend and the staff at this funeral home is wonderful.

I have wonderful and decent people within my life today. It has been about ten years since I graduated from Federation of Organizations in Patchogue, New York. In the past ten years, I have stayed in contact with the Director of Community Services at the Federation. She has seen me grow emotionally and mentally and has been a great support to me. I always kept her posted on what good things were going on within my life and still visit with her sometimes.

I still take my car to Goodyear Tire Center, but in Centereach, New York now, because Centereach is closer to Lake Ronkonkoma than Patchogue is. The staff over at there is wonderful to me; they treat me with courtesy and respect and are always happy to see me. They are very decent and honest people and I consider the staff there to be my friends.

Since I moved to The Waterfalls in Lake Ronkonkoma, I have made new friends within the Ronkonkoma area. I got another AA sponsor and I made some new friends in the AA fellowship. A woman who lives right around the corner takes walks with me at The Waterfalls. Certain evenings, we walk to the top of the hill together where the big building is that has the office in it, and there is a beautiful geyser there. Also, there are beautiful trees, plants, and flower on top of that hill.

I have quite a few friends in the Al-Anon Program too. I am very close to Dorothy Reese, and also a lady by the name of Ann. Ann always says to me, "You are in God's hands, Elizabeth." I also still have an Al-Anon sponsor.

Within my lifetime, my brother and I have never gotten close. He still lives in Massachusetts and has three children, two sons and one daughter. I do not see my sister–in-law at all, either, nor do I see my nephews or niece. Through the help of the Al-Anon Program, I have come to accept this situation with my brother, but from time to time, I do speak to some of my cousins over the phone. Sometimes, I speak to June, who lives in Florida; she is seventy-five years old now. I speak to her daughter, Dawn, my second cousin, who is fifty-one now. Dawn also lives in Florida, not far from her mother. I also speak to Doris, who is about sixty-nine years old now. I do have some family, but not a lot of family.

My cousin John lives in Holbrook, New York, which is the next town over from Lake Ronkonkoma, but I never see him, because his wife and I never really were friendly. John is about sixty-seven now; he has three children, two daughters and one son.

After I moved to The Waterfalls, I started to attend Saint Joseph's Roman Catholic Church in Ronkonkoma. It is the most beautiful Catholic church that I have ever attended in my whole life. I really like the pastor there because he and I agree on some very personal issues. This church prints out beautiful bulletins for Sundays for the parishioners, and within the weekly bulletins is a big prayer list and I have had some of my cousins who I speak with put on the prayer list. My cousins June and Doris are not well physically and need a lot of prayer.

Every day, when I drive into The Waterfalls, I feel as if I am driving into God's Kingdom and I feel extremely close to God there, to the Lord, and to the Blessed Virgin Mary. Every morning, I wake up to see the woods outside of my bedroom windows; the birds start singing at about 4:30 a.m. The first thing I do after I get up in the morning is thank God that I am alive today, sane, and sober. I then pray my rosary and I ask for God's Will in my life, and I pray for my family and a lot of other people. I get such peace, serenity, and joy when I say my rosary. In the evenings, before I go to bed, I pray my rosary again. I always looked upon the Blessed Virgin Mary as being my real mother, because my birth mother was too ill to parent me the right way.

I forgive my parents for everything they have done to me, because my parents were both very ill and both of them had horrible childhoods. My mother's parents both died when she was just a child and she was raised in orphanages. My mother was beaten in those orphanages. My father's father use to beat him.

I feel that both of my parents are praying for me. I see them in a different light now and know that they are healed of their afflictions. They are in a different dimension, and this dimension, or Heaven, is all about love. I feel that my parents have asked for my forgiveness. I have never felt such a connection to both of my parents as I do now. I feel very close to them and look forward to being united with them someday in Heaven.

I have cablevision at home and one of my favorite channels is Cartoon Network; my favorite cartoons are on *The Looney Tunes Show.* This show is on during certain evenings, and Cartoon Network is on Channel 32. On *The Looney Tunes Show,* my favorite cartoon characters are Bugs Bunny, Tweety, and Road Runner. When I watch these cartoons, I sit on the living room couch and laugh. I enjoy cartoons more now than when I was a child. I also watch Nicktoons on Channel 122, which has cartoons and also animated shows. In spite of everything I have been through in my life, I still have a great sense of humor.

Even though I have been through years of mental health treatment and have attended AA and Al-Anon for many years now, I still live with nervous symptoms every day, but I accept it. Doctor Low, the founder of Recovery Inc., now called Recovery International, said that we may never be symptom-free. Some of the nervous symptoms that I experience daily are restlessness, anxiety, shaking, nervousness, and sometimes, I still even have delusions, but I know that they are delusions. I do not have hallucinations today at all. What I mean by delusions is, for example, every time I hear a police car siren, I immediately feel that the police are coming to get me, because I have been taken to the Psychiatric Emergency Services at Stony Brook University twice. But, intellectually, I know that it is just a delusion and dismiss the thought.

I am very proud of myself, because I worked hard at jobs for many years of my life, between the ages of eighteen and sixty, with chronic mental illness. I do plan on going back to work in the near future, as I am looking for work again. I am nearing sixty-two years old. I am not sure of what I will be doing at my next job. But, I know that I will find work. I always did find work in the past. Doctor Low says, "What we did once, we can do again and again."

I chose for now not to work with the mentally ill, because on my last job through the Human Services Agency, I became too emotionally involved with them, to the point where it was hurting me. I felt so sorry for them and I had difficulty handling their behaviors and their temper tantrums at times. My work with the mentally ill was a little too stressful for me. Maybe in the future, I would consider working with them again when I am older and stronger.

I plan on receiving my Bachelor's Degree in History from Stony Brook State University a couple of years from now and getting a part-time job that I will really enjoy. I will probably love that job. I am seriously considering on going into acting such as acting in plays, as I want to do something that I will enjoy. This has become a passion for me and I need to fulfill that passion. I would like to retire at the age of sixty-five, but still work part-time, because I do enjoy working, especially at something which I enjoy. I also plan on living at The Waterfalls forever.

I still do inner child work daily as I talk to my inner child. I tell her how much I love her and that I will always protect her. The wounding that I have lived with all of my life seems to be much better.

On Friday, July 26, 2013, I celebrated my twenty-eight years of sobriety. I feel that I am sober by the grace of God. When I first came into AA in 1985, I had a serious mental disorder. That is no longer true.

Yes, it has been quite a journey and every morning, after I take my shower, I look at myself in the mirror and say to myself, "I love you, Elizabeth, and I am so proud of you."

I even learned to love my name, Elizabeth, and love to be called by my birth name now.

In the Big Book of Alcoholics Anonymous, Chapter Five, the first sentence reads, "Rarely have we seen a person fail who has thoroughly followed our path." Also, every single day of my life, I say the Serenity Prayer: "God, grant me the Serenity to accept the things I cannot change, the courage to change the things I can, and wisdom to know the difference."

Self-Help Mental Health Programs

Recovery International, Doctor Abraham Low's Self-Help Systems
For help in the United States, call the toll-free number 866-221-0302

TWELVE STEP PROGRAMS TOLL-FREE NUMBERS AND WEBSITES

FOR HELP IN THE UNITED STATES:

ALCOHOLICS ANONYMOUS
877-515-1255
www.aa.org

AL-ANON
888-425-2666
www.al-anon.org

SEX AND LOVE ADDICTS ANONYMOUS
www.slaafws.org

OVEREATERS ANONYMOUS
www.oa.org

www.ingramcontent.com/pod-product-compliance
Lightning Source LLC
Chambersburg PA
CBHW071848020426
42331CB00007B/1916